Jayne Netley Mayhew's
Cross Stitch *safari*

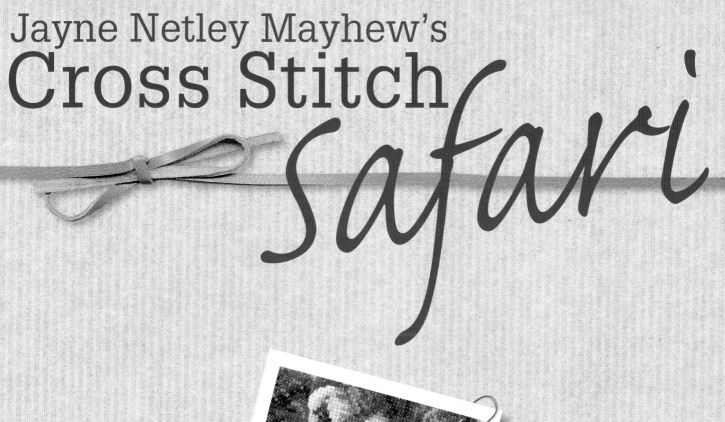

D&C
David and Charles

For Ian, and the people who work so hard to bring us another step closer to knowing and loving Africa.

A DAVID & CHARLES BOOK
Copyright © David & Charles Limited 2006

David & Charles is an F+W Publications Inc. company
4700 East Galbraith Road
Cincinnati, OH 45236

First published in the UK in 2006

Text and illustrations copyright © Jayne Netley Mayhew 2006

Jayne Netley Mayhew has asserted her right to be identified as author of this work
in accordance with the Copyright, Designs and Patents Act, 1988.

A catalogue record for this book is available from the British Library.

ISBN-13: 978-0-7153-2175-1 hardback
ISBN-10: 0-7153-2175-7 hardback

ISBN-13: 978-0-7153-2504-9 paperback
ISBN-10: 0-7153-2504-3 paperback

Printed in Singapore by KHL Printing Co Pte Ltd
for David & Charles
Brunel House   Newton Abbot   Devon

Executive Editor Cheryl Brown
Editor Jennifer Proverbs
Art Editor Prudence Rogers
Designer Charly Bailey
Project Editor Lin Clements
Production Controller Ros Napper
Photographer Kim Sayer

Visit our website at www.davidandcharles.co.uk

David & Charles books are available from all good bookshops; alternatively you can contact our
Orderline on 0870 9908222 or write to us at FREEPOST EX2 110, D&C Direct, Newton Abbot, TQ12 4ZZ
(no stamp required UK only); US customers call 800-289-0963 and Canadian customers call 800-840-5220.

Contents

Into Africa . . .

This book is based on an experience of a lifetime – a glorious African safari, which was planned to coincide with my birthday, my husband Ian's 50th birthday and our 25th wedding anniversary. This journey took us back to a place strong in our memories, a country we had first visited 15 years ago. Africa is like no other place on earth, rich with never-ending sources of wildlife, culture and atmosphere, and so inspiring for me as an artist. So, through my cross stitch embroideries let me take you with me on my fabulous safari, from Kenya's Masai Mara National Reserve to the Serengeti National Park in Tanzania, and a little bit beyond. . .

Painting in the Serengeti

We set out from Heathrow Airport one cloudy afternoon in July and ten hours later were in Nairobi, Kenya. The next morning, under brilliant blue skies, the sun already toasting our skin, we stowed our bags in the Bedford truck that would be our home for the next five weeks. Then we were off to Lake Nakuru where we made our first camp.

I have so many memories of all the magnificent animals, birds and places we saw during our safari that it was difficult to choose subjects for this book. Ngorongoro Crater in Tanzania in particular was a wondrous place. The steep edges of the crater are lush with tropical forest and looking down into the immense crater, which is filled with vast plains and lakes, is a spectacular sight. It was here that we saw black rhinos. Africa has two types of rhinoceros – the black and the white – both endangered species. We were lucky enough to also see white rhinos while on a game drive in Lake Nakuru National Park, Kenya.

We were thrilled to observe plenty of the big cats during our trip, including lions, cheetahs

Could these brothers be more relaxed?

and leopards. They look magnificent but of course are wild and unpredictable. Lying in our tent at night listening to the roar of a nearby lion was an exciting but unnerving experience.

We went on many exciting game drives, our guides pointing out everything of interest. They showed us migration routes that wildebeest have followed for decades, the stones on the river banks worn smooth by the herds. Vast numbers cross at specific points and not only risk being trampled but have to face hungry crocodiles. We also saw massive herds of water buffalo, some feeding along river beds, some just standing chewing cud in the welcome shade of acacia trees.

One memory I treasure is the sight of a baby elephant walking with its mother and aunts among the golden grasses of the savannah. He was simply delightful, touching his mother's flank from time to time as if for reassurance. He gave the impression that he didn't quite know what to do with his trunk, first swinging it in circles, then up and down, ears flapping and head nodding.

During our safari we saw birds in their thousands, including hummingbirds, cattle egrets, fish eagles, vultures, pelicans and flamingos. Pelicans and flamingos seem comfortable companions: both birds are large in body and wing, with oddly shaped beaks and favour the shallow waters of soda lakes for their feeding grounds.

On the bank of the Zambezi – truly African style!

Visiting the Maasai was a highlight of our trip. Maa-sai means 'my people' and they truly are a noble nation. The welcoming dance of the warriors is a memory that will stay with me forever. We were invited to join them one evening and as we gathered around the campfire a rumble like thunder came from the distance. It grew louder and louder and then the warriors appeared from the darkness in their full glory, stamping their feet and chanting with a rhythmic, guttural sound that sent tingles down my spine. They danced, still chanting, forming circles and weaving around and then leapt high into the air with whoops of joy. The sight was exhilarating and awesome.

Flat Dog camp in South Luangwa National Park, Zambia, was one of my personal highlights. It was my birthday and in the morning I was greeted by our guide Chris with 'happy birthday old woman' (a compliment, I later found out). Unbeknown to me, the group had cooked me a special birthday dinner – roast beef and all the trimmings, followed by a chocolate cake covered in candles. We were just preparing to eat, when into camp walked an elephant. He began feeling around for food with his trunk but found a bottle of vegetable oil instead. He picked it up, found he couldn't open it, put it back down and very deliberately stood on it, which drew groans from our cook Johannes. The rest of the meal was a delight, the elephant reappearing every now and again – a truly wonderful birthday memory.

Our secluded and romantic nest!

Welcoming dance of Maasai warriors

Of course, we only saw a fraction of the fabulous landscapes that make up the intoxicating country of Africa, but from my safari I have brought you a taste of the diverse range of animals that this land is home to, and wish you many hours of enjoyable stitching.

Lions

A highlight of our safari was being in the middle of a lion hunt while on a game drive in the Masai Mara. We watched with bated breath as three lionesses worked their way around us and a herd of Thompson gazelle. Slowly they move in closer, each taking turns to manoeuvre into position. It was exhilarating and frightful: one moment wishing the gazelles would spot them and run; the next thinking, slowly, slowly lioness or they'll spot you. The end came fast for the gazelle – from flight to death in seconds. Then four more lions emerged from concealment in the grass – they had been blocking the escape route and we hadn't even seen them.

Kings of Africa

Stitch count 142 x 200
Design size 25.7 x 36.3cm (10⅛ x 14¼in)

You will need
- 40.5 x 51cm (16 x 20in) sand 28-count linen
- DMC stranded cotton (floss) as listed in chart key (1 skein of each colour)
- Tapestry needle size 24–26

Prepare your fabric and mark the centre point (see page 100). Work outwards from the centre of the chart on pages 8–11. Work over two threads of linen, using two strands of stranded cotton (floss) for all cross stitch. Work the backstitch with one strand of black around eyes, nose and mouth detail. Work French knots using one strand of white for eye highlights. Once all stitching is complete, mount and frame the picture (see page 103 for advice).

These two adult male lions are in their prime. Together they form a coalition, where they will share mating rights with the females in the pride and defend a large area against other males.

Top Left

8 Lions

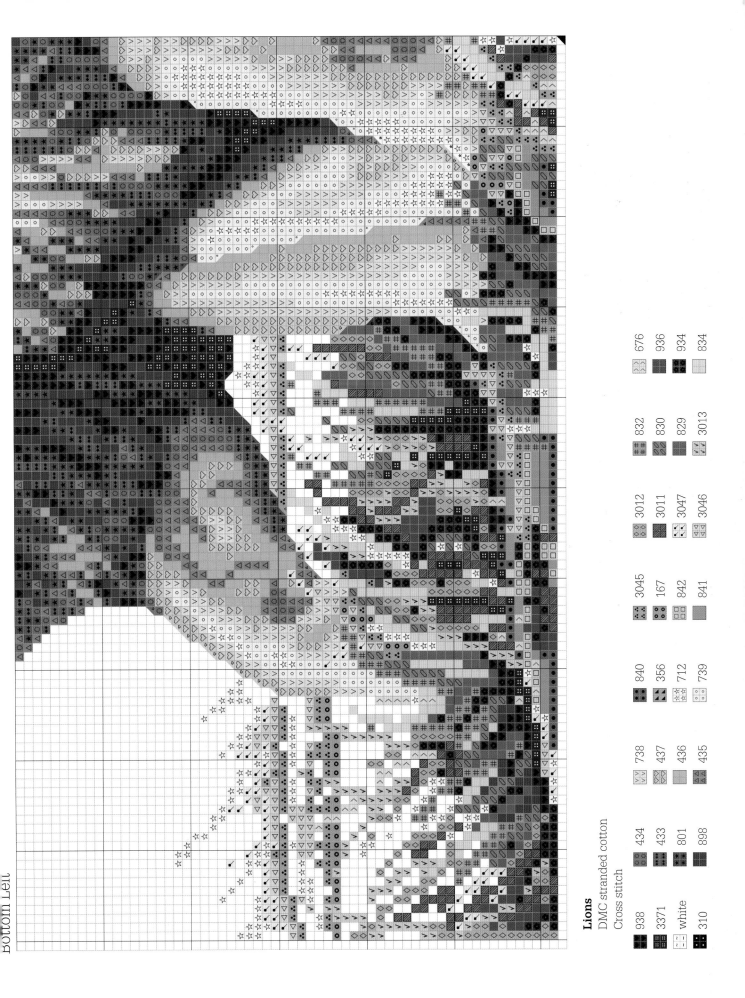

Lions

DMC stranded cotton
Cross stitch

676	936	934	834
832	830	829	3013
3012	3011	3047	3046
3045	167	842	841
840	356	712	739
738	437	436	435
434	433	801	898
938	3371	white	310

10 Lions

Lions
DMC stranded cotton
Cross stitch

938	676
3371	936
white	934
310	834
434	832
433	830
801	829
898	3013
738	3012
437	3011
436	3047
435	3046
840	3045
356	167
712	842
739	841

Lions 11

Elephants

Elephants truly are magnificent, and to watch the females gently taking care of the young is heart-warming. During a close encounter with an elephant, I was able to look closely at its skin and was amazed at how rough it was – like a quilt covered with hard bristle. Their brown eyes are full of intelligence, the eyelashes long and as thick as wire. While he and I looked at each other his trunk was gently searching for the food I had in a pouch.

Giants of the Plains

Stitch count 120 x 180
Design size 21.7 x 32.6cm (8½ x 12¾in)

You will need
- 35.5 x 46cm (14 x 18in) sky blue 14-count Aida
- DMC stranded cotton (floss) as listed in chart key (1 skein of each colour and 2 skeins of 844, 645, 646 and 647)
- Tapestry needle size 24–26

Prepare your fabric and mark the centre point (see page 100). Work outwards from the centre of the chart overleaf. Work over one block of Aida, using two strands of stranded cotton (floss) for all cross stitch. Once all stitching is complete, mount and frame your picture (see page 103 for advice).

I nearly lost my birthday tea to an elephant, who entered the campsite to snuffle around the campfire in search of food. Luckily, my chocolate birthday cake was safe in the lorry!

Elephants 13

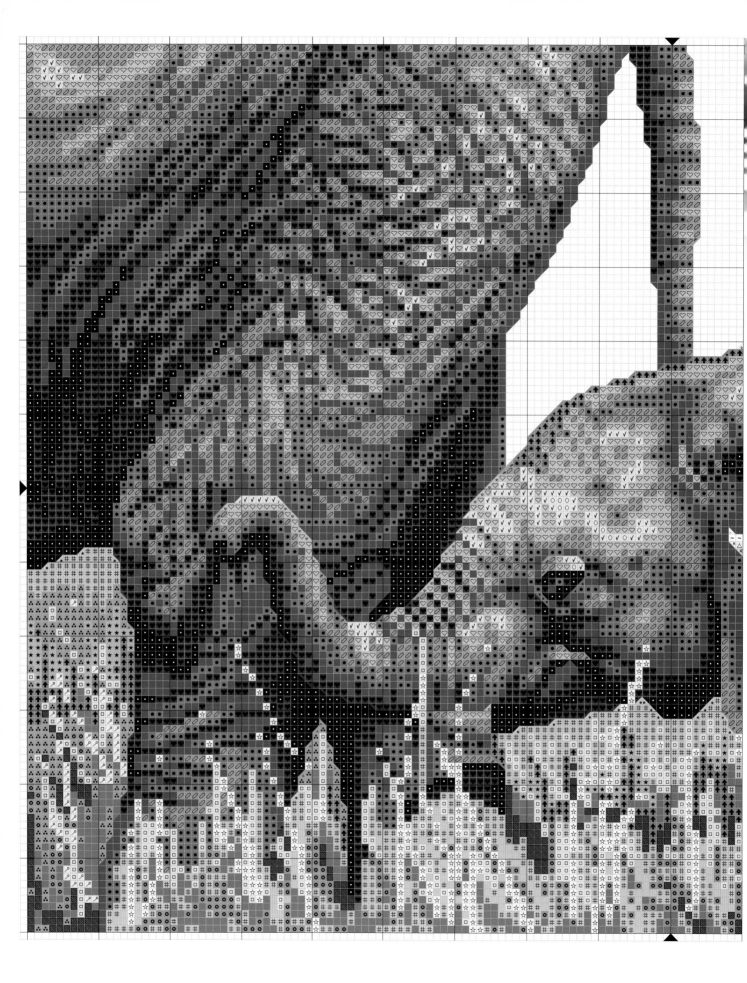

14 Elephants

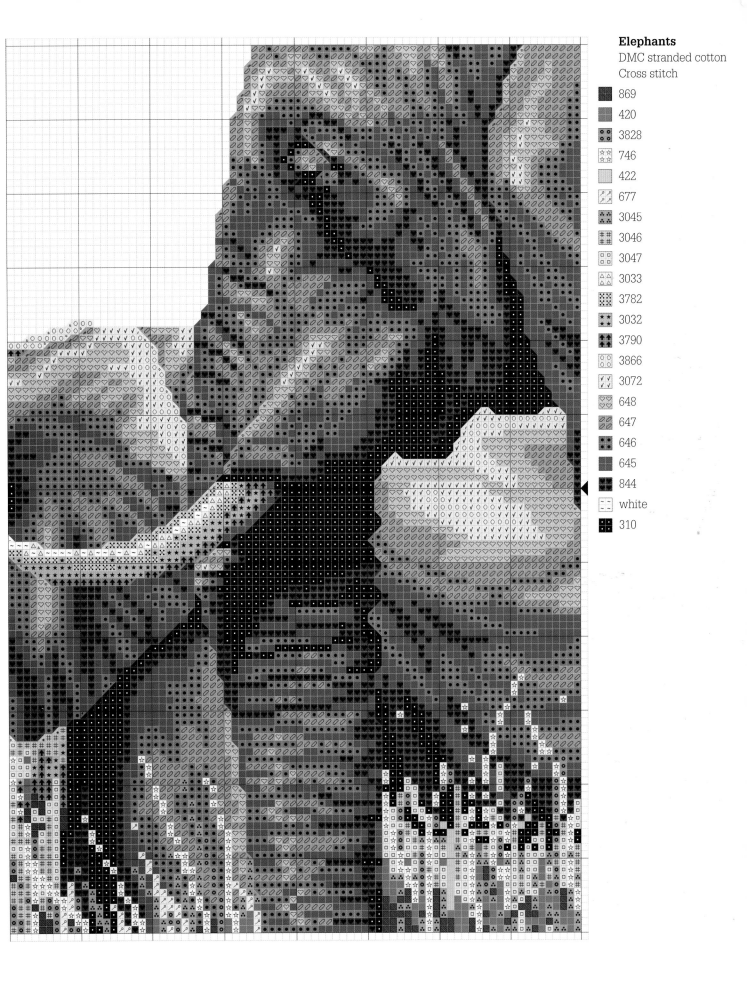

	869
	420
	3828
	746
	422
	677
	3045
	3046
	3047
	3033
	3782
	3032
	3790
	3866
	3072
	648
	647
	646
	645
	844
	white
	310

Chimpanzee

When you're really up close and personal with a chimpanzee, as I was with this old boy, you can be in no doubt that they are our closest relative in the animal kingdom. Their intelligence, emotion and communication skills shine out. I called him 'the thinker', as his look said it all – he's seen it, heard it and done it all before, and was studying us as much as we were studying him!

The Thinker

Stitch count 122 x 120
Design size 22 x 21.75cm (8¾ x 8½in)

You will need
- 36 x 33cm (14 x 13in) natural 14-count Aida
- DMC stranded cotton (floss) as listed in chart key (1 skein of each colour and 2 skeins of 452)
- Tapestry needle size 24–26

Prepare your fabric and mark the centre point (see page 100). Work outwards from the centre of the chart overleaf. Work over one block of Aida, using two strands of stranded cotton (floss) for all cross stitch. Work the backstitch with one strand of black for the eyes, nose and mouth detail. Once all the stitching is complete, mount and frame your picture (see page 103 for advice).

The artist in me is fascinated by the fact that the arm of a human and chimpanzee and a dolphin's flipper, though looking very different, all contain the same arrangement of bones.

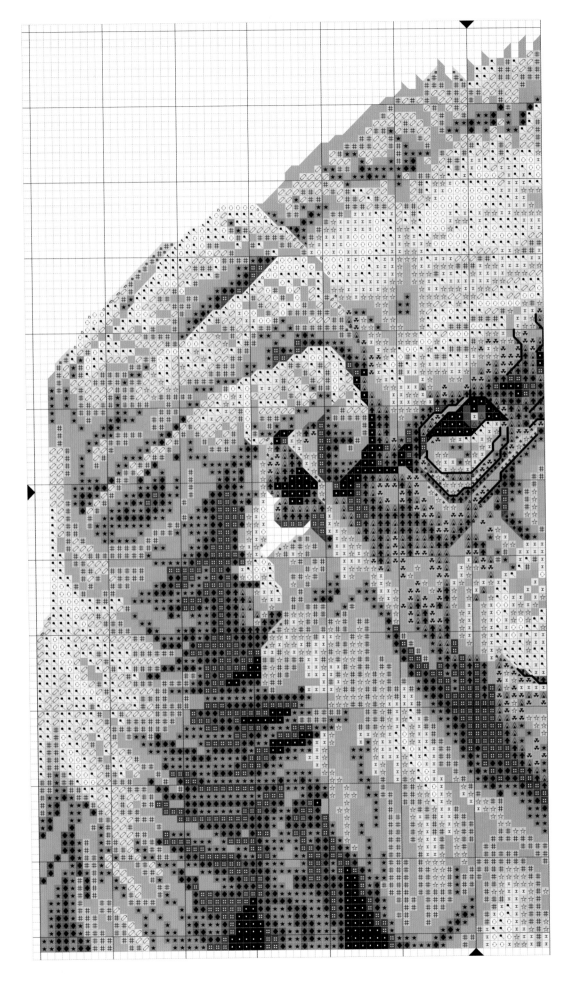

18 Chimpanzee

Chimpanzee
DMC stranded cotton
Cross stitch

▦	433
■	938
I I	453
☆	452
	451
❖	3861
▲	3860
▦	779
◌	3866
∴	3024
⬦⬦	415
# #	318
	414
★	317
◆	413
▦	3799
■	310

Chimpanzee 19

Wildebeest

Robert, one of the crew who looked after us on safari, told us how the wildebeest got its name. When God made the animals he had lots of bits left over so he put these together and when asked what this animal should be called, he said 'wild beast', and so the wildebeest was formed. It certainly is an ungainly creature to look at but despite the losses during migration it is one of the most successful animals on the African plains.

Migration Crossing

Stitch count 200 x 200
Design size 36.3 x 36.3cm (14¼ x 14¼in)

You will need
- 48 x 48cm (19 x 19in) sky blue 14-count Aida
- DMC stranded cotton (floss) as listed in chart key (1 skein of each colour, 2 skeins of white, 838, 840 and 841 and 4 skeins of 310)
- Tapestry needle size 24–26

Prepare your fabric and mark the centre point (see page 100). Work outwards from the centre of the chart on pages 22–25. Work over one block of Aida, using two strands of stranded cotton (floss) for all cross stitch. Once all stitching is complete, mount and frame your picture (see page 103 for advice).

The sheer number of wildebeest on migration is astounding, forming an endless black line across the plains. It's all movement, noise and dust, with males running back and forth to hassle the females along.

Wildebeest
DMC stranded cotton
Cross stitch

470	3768	371	801	842	838	642	white
648	926	372	938	841	ecru	640	310
3072	677	3045	3371	840	822	3787	
924	370	167	543	839	644	3021	

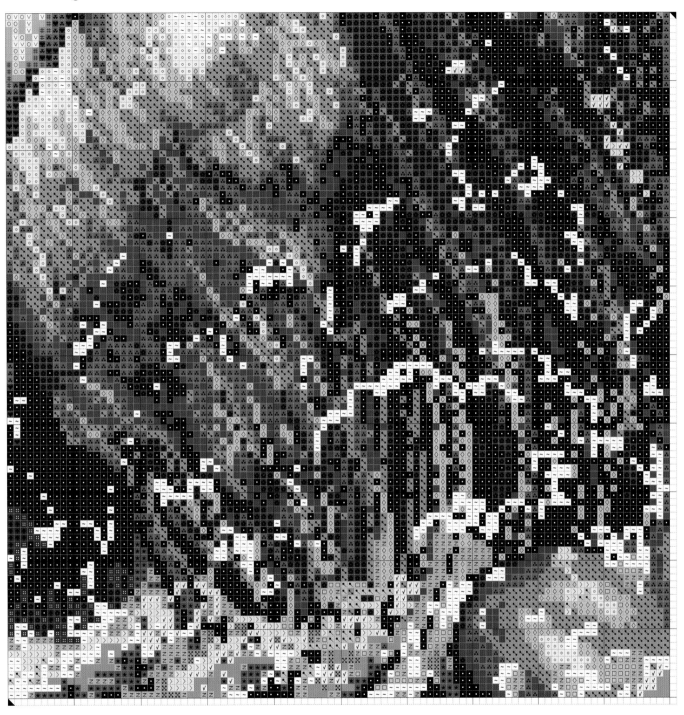

Wildebeest

DMC stranded cotton
Cross stitch

470	3768	371	801	842	838	642	white
648	926	372	938	841	ecru	640	310
3072	677	3045	3371	840	822	3787	
924	370	167	543	839	644	3021	

Impala

These wonderful doe-eyed antelopes are a delight to watch and are such lovely creatures, full of grace and spirit. As they graze, they are ever watchful, frequently raising their heads to look around, ready to flee at a moment's notice at any sign or movement of a predator. And there are many of these – lions, leopards and wild dogs to name but a few. Given the chance, even baboons will take a young impala calf. It was with pounding hearts that we watched a lioness stalk an impala. I wanted to cry out a warning, but was also willing the lioness to succeed: nature can seem so cruel at times.

Flight of Fancy

Stitch count 160 x 110
Design size 29 x 20cm (11½ x 7⅝in)

You will need
- 43 x 33cm (17 x 13in) sage green 14-count Aida
- DMC stranded cotton (floss) as listed in chart key (1 skein of each colour)
- Tapestry needle size 24–26

Prepare your fabric and mark the centre point (see page 100). Work outwards from the centre of the chart overleaf. Work over one block of Aida, using two strands of stranded cotton (floss) for all cross stitch. Work the French knot with one strand of white for the eye highlight. Once all stitching is complete, mount and frame your picture (see page 103 for advice).

In the dry season, impala form mixed herds but when the mating season begins the bachelor males form groups of their own and compete for territories and females.

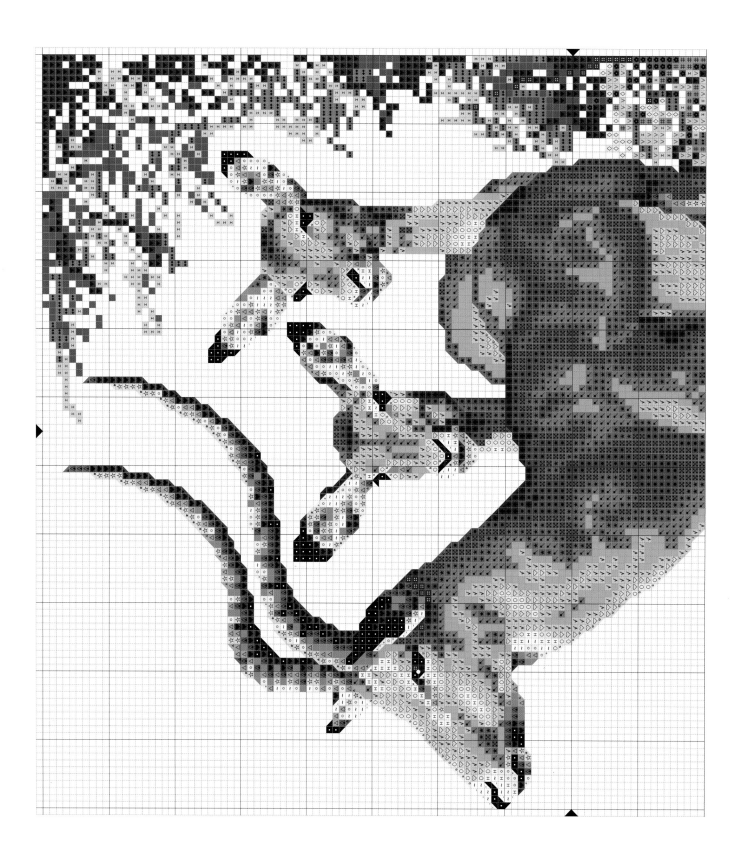

28 Impala

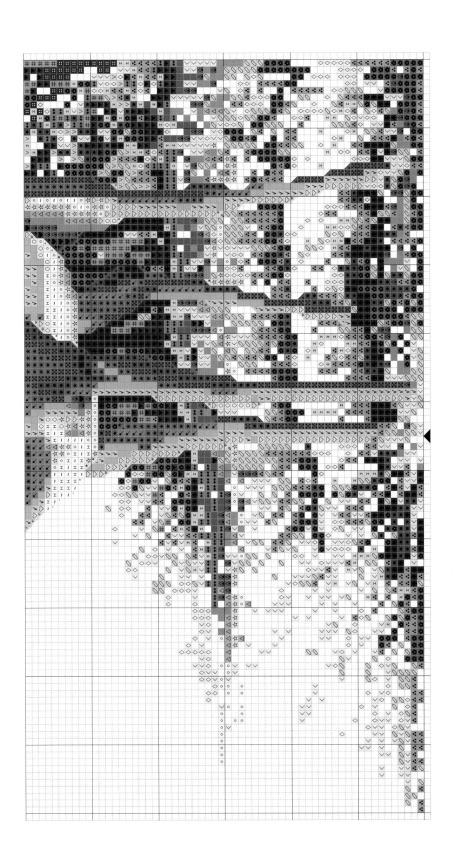

Impala
DMC stranded cotton
Cross stitch

738	433	644	472	832	677
739	434	822	3021	834	3045
712	435	3371	3787	934	3046
white	436	938	640	937	3047
310	437	801	642	470	829

Cheetahs

On our fourth day of safari we saw this wonderful pair of young cheetahs waiting for their mother to return from hunting. They still had their fluffy kitten hair, which disappears as they mature. When it's time to leave the family group the young often stay together, the females finally leaving when impelled by the instinct to breed. This young cat was lying in the shade of some scrub in the Masai Mara, unconcerned about our clicking cameras. His brother joined him and with a yawn he rolled on to his back and stretched out, their hind legs tangling, comfortable with each other. The only sign that they were aware of us was an occasional twitch of the tail and a lazy glance.

Waiting for Mother

Stitch count 260 x 190
Design size 47 x 34.5cm (18½ x 13½in)

You will need
- 61 x 46cm (24 x 18in) sky blue 28-count linen
- DMC stranded cotton (floss) as listed in chart key (1 skein of each colour and 2 skeins of white, 677 and 746)
- Tapestry needle size 24–26

Prepare your fabric and mark the centre point (see page 100). Work outwards from the centre of the chart on pages 32–35. Stitch the foreground area first (cheetahs and grasses), working over two threads of linen, using two strands of stranded cotton (floss) for all cross stitch. Then work the background landscape using one strand of colours 3045, 3046, 3047, 611 and 746. Work the backstitch grass detail with a mixture of 801, 676 and 677 and French knots grass detail with one strand of 676. Work the whiskers in white long stitch in one strand (shown in black on the chart). Once all stitching is complete, mount and frame your picture (see page 103 for advice).

I love the cheetah's markings – the long tear-drop shaped lines on each side of the nose are so recognizable, there is no mistaking this handsome cat.

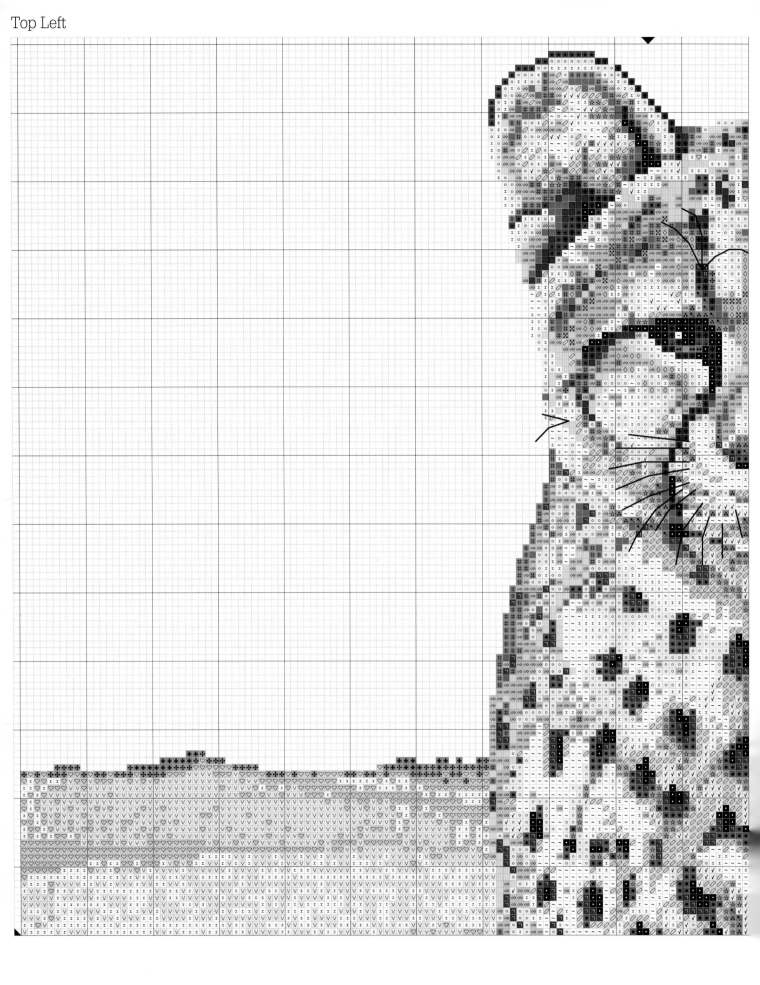

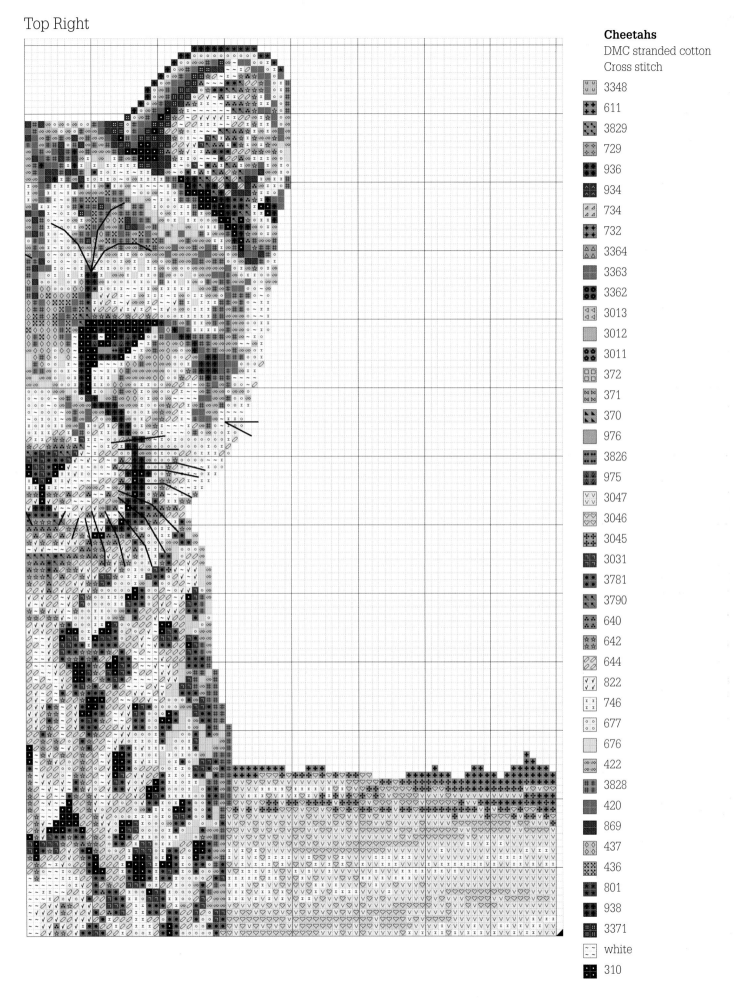

Cheetahs
DMC stranded cotton
Cross stitch

⊔⊔	3348
✚✚	611
▨▨	3829
✕✕	729
▦▦	936
�ΛΛ	934
◁◁	734
✦✦	732
△△	3364
▨▨	3363
▨▨	3362
◁◁	3013
▨▨	3012
▨▨	3011
▢▢	372
⋈⋈	371
◣◣	370
▨	976
▦▦	3826
▲▲	975
⋁⋁	3047
♡♡	3046
✛✛	3045
⊞⊞	3031
●●	3781
◥◥	3790
⁚⁚	640
☆☆	642
⧄⧄	644
⋁⋁	822
ΙΙ	746
∘∘	677
▢	676
∞∞	422
＃＃	3828
▨	420
▨	869
◇◇	437
▩▩	436
✱✱	801
▨	938
▦▦	3371
⁚⁚	white
▨▨	310

34 Cheetahs

Cheetahs
DMC stranded cotton
Cross stitch

Symbol	Color
	3348
	611
	3829
	729
	936
	934
	734
	732
	3364
	3363
	3362
	3013
	3012
	3011
	372
	371
	370
	976
	3826
	975
	3047
	3046
	3045
	3031
	3781
	3790
	640
	642
	644
	822
	746
	677
	676
	422
	3828
	420
	869
	437
	436
	801
	938
	3371
	white
	310

Flamingos

Flamingos are beautiful birds, with their pink, red and white colouring and long legs and necks. They form huge, sociable flocks, a haze of pink at the edge of soda lakes. At breeding time thousands perform synchronized courtship dances and their formation flying is a lovely sight. Each day they have to drink and bathe in fresh water, a massed flurry of pink and white.

A Sea of Pink

Stitch count 110 x 180
Design size 20 x 33cm (7¾ x 13in)

You will need
- 33 x 46cm (13 x 18in) white 14-count Aida
- DMC stranded cotton (floss) as listed in chart key (1 skein of each colour)
- Tapestry needle size 24–26

Prepare your fabric and mark the centre point (see page 100). Work outwards from the centre of the chart overleaf. Work over one block of Aida, using two strands of stranded cotton (floss) for all cross stitch. Once all stitching is complete, mount and frame your picture (see page 103 for advice).

A peaceful scene of feeding flamingos, with the golden glow of afternoon and pink reflections on a shimmering soda lake, bring back wonderful memories of Africa.

38 Flamingos

Flamingos
DMC stranded cotton
Cross stitch

△△	453
☆☆	452
••	3861
▦	3860
▦	779
I I	762
▷▷	415
⁝⁝	318
◖◗	414
▦	317
▦	413
▦	3799
√√	3727
♡♡	3726
▦	315
▦	902
▦	3685
▦	777
★★	3831
▦	961
##	962
◇◇	3716
◣◢	963
∘∘	818
⌐⌐	white
▦	310

Water Buffalo

One of Africa's 'big five', the water buffalo is a large and impressive beast. We were lucky to see several herds in the Masai Mara and the Serengeti. They never range far from a watercourse, as they need to drink daily. One afternoon we watched a vast herd graze their way along a riverbed under the cover of trees, among the shrubs and lush green grass – a mass of bodies, bellows and movement, ears and tails swishing the flies away. The females and young were flanked by the males who are much bigger, with a set of robust horns that meet in a boss on their foreheads. Not an animal to trifle with!

Armed and Dangerous

Stitch count 105 x 180
Design size 19 x 32.7cm (7½ x 13in)

You will need
- 33 x 46cm (13 x 18in) sage green 14-count Aida
- DMC stranded cotton (floss) as listed in chart key (1 skein of each colour)
- Tapestry needle size 24–26

Prepare your fabric and mark the centre point (see page 100). Work outwards from the centre of the chart overleaf. Work over one block of Aida, using two strands of stranded cotton (floss) for all cross stitch. Work the backstitch with one strand of black for the eye detail. Once all stitching is complete, mount and frame your picture (see page 103 for advice).

While driving along a trail in the Serengeti, we attracted the interest of some water buffalo. As we passed them, one in particular seemed to say 'don't mess with me'.

Water Buffalo 41

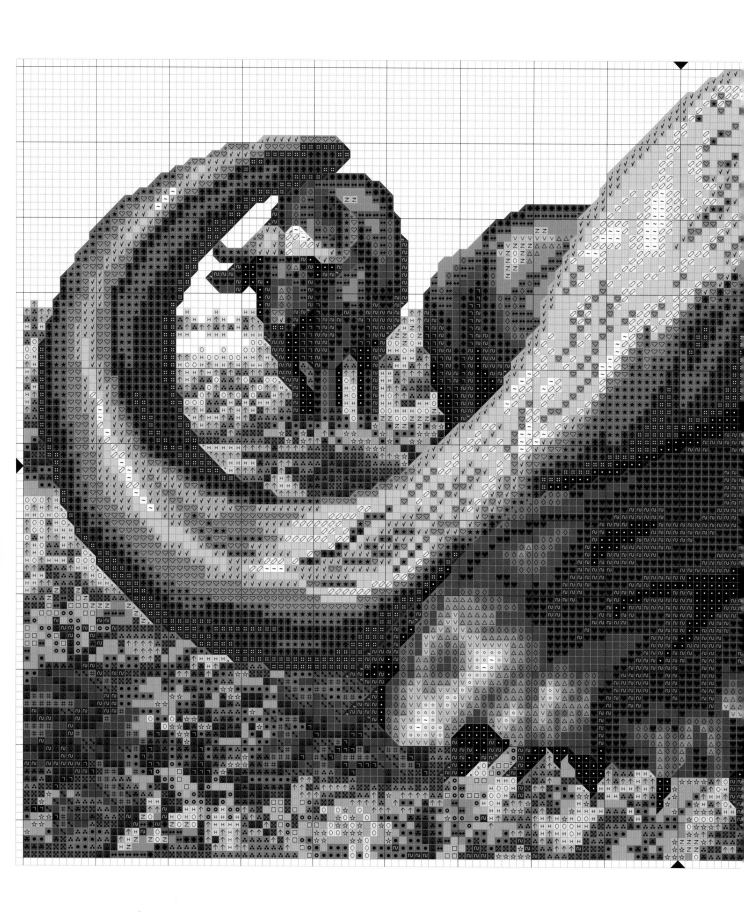

42 Water Buffalo

Water Buffalo
DMC stranded cotton
Cross stitch

ᴴᴴᴴ	613
↑↑↑	612
	611
	610
	372
	371
	370
	3053
	3052
	3051
	3011
	470
	937
	936
	934
	433
	801
	938
	3371
	3866
ᶻᶻ	842
	841
	840
	839
	3021
	762
	415
✓✓	318
	414
	317
	413
	3799
	3072
ⱽⱽ	648
	647
	646
	645
	844
	white
	310

Water Buffalo 43

The Maasai

The Maasai are a noble nation: once a nomadic people, they are beginning to have more permanent settlements. Some boys are now sent to school to be educated and keep up with changing times. Work is strictly divided between men and women. The men govern, raise cattle and protect the settlement and livestock from animals. Women's work includes the building of huts and domestic duties. They shave and polish theirs heads, unlike the young men, whose long hair is a sign of beauty. Red is a favourite colour in Maasai clothing, in various tones and patterns. They dress simply, with material tied at the shoulder and draped over. Metal bangles are worn on arms and legs, while bands and bead pendants adorn their heads, ankles and earlobes. The circlets and strings of beads around their necks give them a look of great elegance and beauty.

Warrior and Lady

Stitch count (for each design) 218 x 80
Design size 39.4 x 14.5cm (15½ x 5¾in)

You will need (for each design)
- 53 x 28cm (21 x 11in) blue 28-count linen
- DMC stranded cotton (floss) as listed in chart key (1 skein of each colour)
- Tapestry needle size 24–26

The stitching instructions are the same for both portraits. Although shown together, opposite, they have been designed to be framed individually as shown on page 103. Prepare your fabric and mark the centre point (see page 100). Work outwards from the centre of the charts on pages 46–49. Work over two threads of linen, using two strands of stranded cotton (floss) for all cross stitch. Once all stitching is complete, mount and frame your picture (see page 103 for advice).

In the darkness we could hear them coming from some distance: with thunder in their feet and a rhythmic chant of guttural sounds, the warriors appeared to perform their welcoming dance – the spirit of the Maasai in its most evocative form.

46 The Maasai

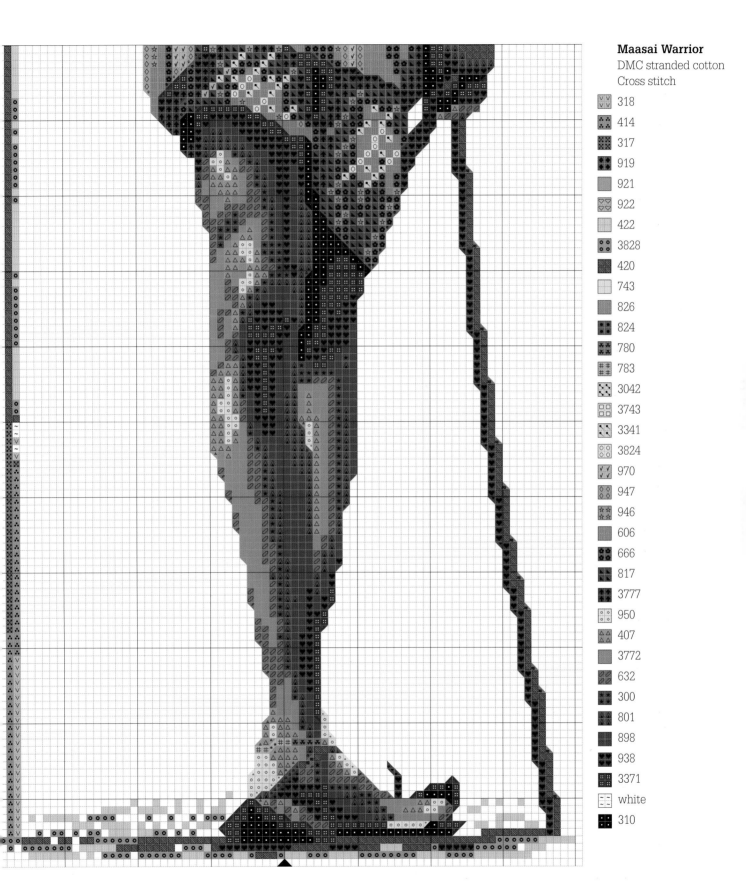

Maasai Warrior
DMC stranded cotton
Cross stitch

318
414
317
919
921
922
422
3828
420
743
826
824
780
783
3042
3743
3341
3824
970
947
946
606
666
817
3777
950
407
3772
632
300
801
898
938
3371
white
310

The Maasai 47

48 The Maasai

Maasai Lady
DMC stranded cotton
Cross stitch

	422
	3828
	420
	666
	311
	3842
	517
	922
	921
	920
	919
	918
	3042
	3743
	780
	783
	743
	162
	813
	826
	824
	712
	739
	351
	606
	304
	950
	407
	3772
	632
	300
	801
	898
	938
	3371
	white
	310

Rhinoceros

It's only when you get close to a rhino that you appreciate just how large they are. On a game drive in Lake Nakuru National Park, Kenya, we saw a magnificent white rhino having a wallow in a mud hole. Only later, as I spotted other mud wallows much further into the bush, did I realize how lucky we were to see this endangered animal doing what comes naturally. Later in our trip we were thrilled to see black rhino in the Ngorongoro Crater, in Tanzania.

Rare Giant

Stitch count 110 x 160
Design size 20 x 30cm (7¾ x 11½in)

You will need
- 33 x 43cm (13 x 17in) light grey 14-count Aida
- DMC stranded cotton (floss) as listed in chart key (1 skein of each colour)
- Tapestry needle size 24–26

Prepare your fabric and mark the centre point (see page 100). Work outwards from the centre of the chart overleaf. Work over one block of Aida, using two strands of stranded cotton (floss) for all cross stitch. Work the backstitch with one strand: black for the face detail and 676, 938 and 3051 for the backstitch/long stitch grass detail. Once all stitching is complete, mount and frame your picture (see page 103 for advice).

A mud bath to cool and protect the skin from biting insects, and a few oxpeckers to help remove pests, must be a good way for a rhino to start the day.

Rhinoceros 51

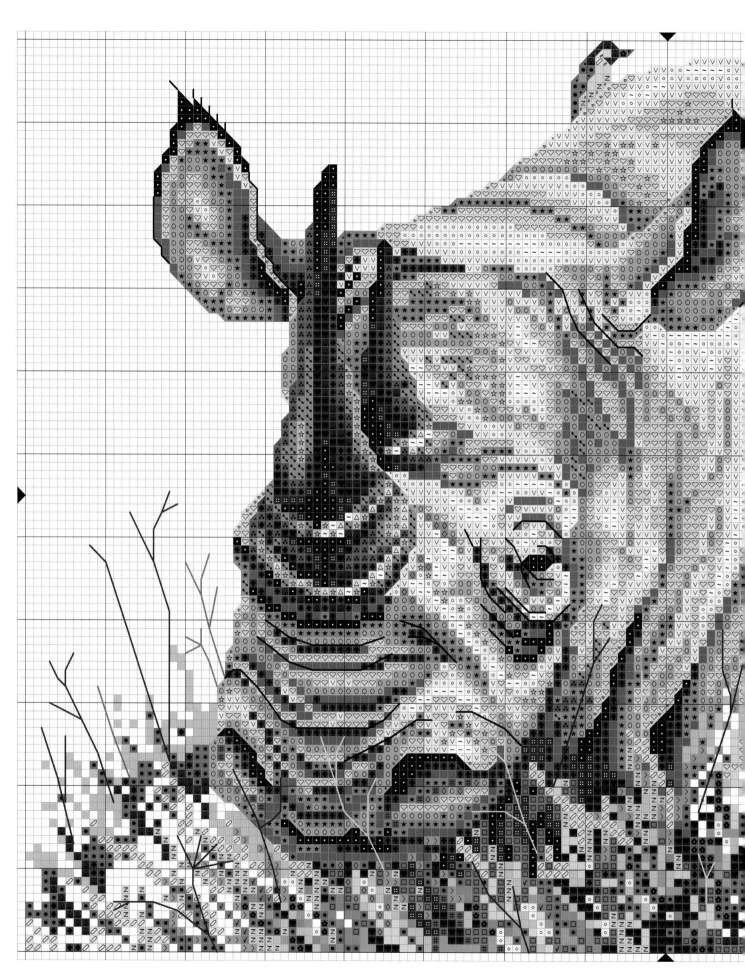

52 Rhinoceros

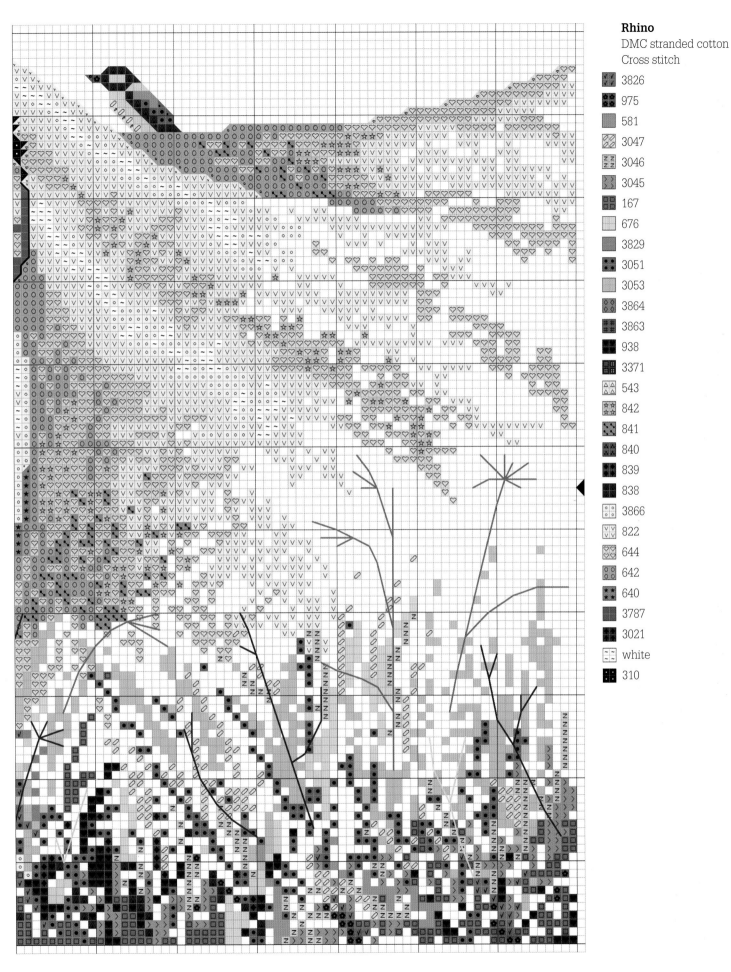

Rhino
DMC stranded cotton
Cross stitch

✓✓	3826
▦	975
▨	581
⊘⊘	3047
ᴢᴢ	3046
⋈	3045
▦	167
▦	676
▦	3829
⬢⬢	3051
▦	3053
▦	3864
▦	3863
▦	938
▦	3371
△△	543
✦✦	842
▦	841
▦	840
▦	839
▦	838
◦◦	3866
✓✓	822
▨▨	644
◦◦	642
★★	640
▦	3787
▦	3021
⊡⊡	white
▦	310

Rhinoceros 53

Fish Eagle

This magnificent eagle is known as the 'voice of Africa', as it throws back its head and gives a loud yelping cry. Easily identified by its striking colouring, it is often seen perching high on branches beside rivers and lakes. On a late evening game drive we stopped to watch the sun go down and on the horizon a lone tree stood in the vast grassland, with a fish eagle perched in the topmost branches. As the sun set, the sky deepening to violet-blue streaked with gold and crimson, the tree and bird were silhouetted against this stunning backdrop. Africa's night-time song of insects and animals sang in our ears and we hardly dared to blink as the sun sank swiftly to the horizon. A magical memory.

Voice of Africa

Stitch count 152 x 110
Design size 27.5 x 20cm (11 x 7¾in)

You will need
- 40.5 x 33cm (16 x 13in) sky blue 14-count Aida
- DMC stranded cotton (floss) as listed in chart key (1 skein of each colour)
- Tapestry needle size 24–26

Prepare your fabric and mark the centre point (see page 100). Work outwards from the centre of the chart overleaf. Work over one block of Aida, using two strands of stranded cotton (floss) for all cross stitch. Work the backstitch with one strand: black around the eye and 317 for the beak detail. Work the French knot with one strand of white for the eye highlight. Once all stitching is complete, mount and frame your picture (see page 103 for advice).

We spotted this fish eagle while on a boat looking at hippos in Lake Naivasha, Kenya. The lake is a haven for birds and among the massed reeds and papyrus we saw many different wading birds. The old moorings were in constant use by cormorants and this wonderful fish eagle.

56 *Fish Eagle*

Fish Eagle
DMC stranded cotton
Cross stitch

739				
782				
780				
733				

732	3768	612	745	435	414
730	926	613	640	434	317
937	927	415	642	433	413
935	928	318	644	801	3799
934	610	743	822	938	white
924	611	744	436	3371	310

Leopard

If the lions are the kings of Africa, then the leopard must be the queen. This exquisite cat takes my breath away. They are so elusive: always two steps behind you or two in front, and very difficult to spot because they blend so well into the undergrowth. The fabulously marked coat is such an effective camouflage that they seem to melt into the grasses and disappear. I have used one of my own paintings as inspiration for this lovely design.

Queen of Cats

Stitch count 199 x 209
Design size 36 x 38cm (14¼ x 15in)

You will need
- 48 x 51cm (19 x 20in) cream 14-count Aida
- DMC stranded cotton (floss) as listed in chart key (1 skein of each colour and 2 skeins of 310 and 677)
- Tapestry needle size 24–26

Prepare your fabric and mark the centre point (see page 100). Work outwards from the centre of the chart on pages 60–63. Work over one block of Aida, using two strands of stranded cotton (floss) for all cross stitch. Work the backstitch with one strand of 801, 520 and 3864 for the grass detail. Work long stitch in one strand of white for the whiskers (shown as grey on the chart). Once all stitching is complete, mount and frame your picture (see page 103 for advice).

While out on a game drive looking for a leopard in Lake Nakuru National Park, he was back at our camp stalking impala. We were alerted by noisy baboons, but only caught a glimpse as he disappeared.

Leopard
DMC stranded cotton
Cross stitch

3864	520	470	832	3046	3033	801	420	3827	white
3863	919	469	831	3045	3782	938	869	977	310
3862	921	937	830	167	3032	3371	712	976	
524	472	834	829	3859	3790	422	677	3826	
522	471	833	3047	3858	3781	3828	676	975	

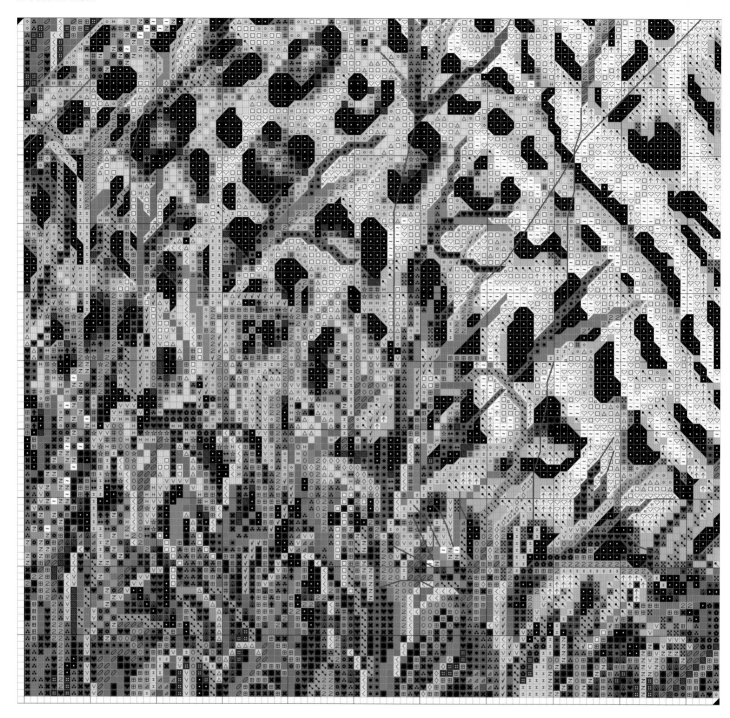

Leopard
DMC stranded cotton
Cross stitch

3864	520	470	832	3046	3033	801	420	3827	white
3863	919	469	831	3045	3782	938	869	977	310
3862	921	937	830	167	3371	3032	712	976	
524	472	834	829	3859	3790	422	677	3826	
522	471	833	3047	3858	3781	3828	676	975	

Paradise Flycatcher

As we journeyed through the diverse African landscapes, including tropical forest, woodland, savannah, rivers and lakes, we saw many fabulous birds. The larger birds, such as herons and ibis, were easy to spot but the smaller breeds were just as rewarding. This beautiful paradise flycatcher was easy to identify by its long chestnut tail feathers, but you have to get closer to see the bright blue bill and eye wattle and the glossy crest. In Africa they often nest in gardens, building a nest in a fork of a tree using bark and fine plant material bound with spiders' webs. The outside of the nest is decorated with lichens to help camouflage it, though it is seldom completely hidden. While sitting on the eggs the male will have his tail feathers gracefully drooping over the edge.

A Graceful Tail

Stitch count 110 x 100
Design size 20 x 18cm (7¾ x 7¼in)

You will need

- 33 x 30.5cm (13 x 12in) sage green 14-count Aida
- DMC stranded cotton (floss) as listed in chart key (1 skein of each colour)
- Tapestry needle size 24–26

Prepare your fabric and mark the centre point (see page 100). Work outwards from the centre of the chart overleaf. Work over one block of Aida, using two strands of stranded cotton (floss) for all cross stitch. Work the backstitch for the bird's legs with two strands of 413. Work remaining backstitch with one strand: black for the eye and beak and 975 and 976 for the backstitch/long stitch tail detail. Work the French knot with two strands of white for the eye highlight. Once all stitching is complete, mount and frame your picture (see page 103 for advice).

Africa is a wonderland for any bird lover. We saw hornbills, kingfishers, bee-eaters, lilac-breasted rollers, hoopoes, barbets, ibis, bustards, weaver birds – and some I still have not been able to identify!

Paradise Flycatcher

DMC stranded cotton
Cross stitch

3046	3348	165	801	976	414	995
3047	840	166	938	3826	317	996
3345	842	320	3371	975	413	white
3346	725	368	3827	415	3818	310
3347	3078	369	977	318	890	

Cattle Egret

DMC stranded cotton
Cross stitch

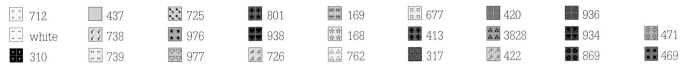

712	437	725	801	169	677	420	936
white	738	976	938	168	413	3828	934	471
310	739	977	726	762	317	422	869	469

Cattle Egret

With their snowy-white plumage and long sinuous necks, egrets are striking birds. In Africa, where there are animals there always seem to be cattle egrets, following along behind the herds, picking up the insects that have been disturbed. They search for grasshoppers and beetles and can also be seen riding on animals' backs, particularly wildebeest, looking for ticks and fleas – and presumably they have the added advantage of height to spot insects among the grasses. We also saw two other types of egrets – the great white egret and the little egret, which are similar to the cattle egret but more heron-like. Cattle egrets prefer a drier terrain. They breed in colonies and roost in trees and bushes, and from a distance a massed flock can make the trees look almost snow-laden.

Following the Footsteps

Stitch count 100 x 105
Design size 18 x 19cm (7¼ x 7½in)

You will need
- 30.5 x 30.5cm (12 x 12in) black 14-count Aida
- DMC stranded cotton (floss) as listed in chart key (1 skein of each colour)
- Tapestry needle size 24–26

Prepare your fabric and mark the centre point (see page 100). Work outwards from the centre of the chart on the previous page. Work over one block of Aida, using two strands of stranded cotton (floss) for all cross stitch. Work the backstitch with one strand: black for the eye and beak and 938, 420 and 677 for the backstitch/long stitch grass detail. Work the French knots in one strand of white for the eye highlight and 677 for the grass details. Once all stitching is complete, mount and frame your picture (see page 103 for advice).

During our safari we frequently saw flocks of cattle egrets following and running in front of a herd of wildebeest, picking off the insects that were disturbed by the grazing animals.

Zebras

While in the Ngorongoro Crater in Tanzania we watched zebras ford a river. They began to drink and cross in small groups but then, in a flurry of panic, bounded to the other side of the river, slipping and sliding through knee-high mud. The next group, after similar agitation, did the same. There seemed to be no apparent danger but the zebra could sense something – were they expecting an attack from the water by a crocodile or from behind by a lion? The feeling of danger was quite tangible, making me feel uneasy too, to the point where I was looking over my shoulder.

Bottoms Up!

Stitch count 110 x 185
Design size 20 x 33.5cm (7¾ x 13¼in)

You will need
- 33 x 46cm (13 x 18in) sage green 14-count Aida
- DMC stranded cotton (floss) as listed in chart key (1 skein of each colour and 3 skeins of 310)
- Tapestry needle size 24–26

Prepare your fabric and mark the centre point (see page 100). Work outwards from the centre of the chart overleaf. Work over one block of Aida, using two strands of stranded cotton (floss) for all cross stitch. Once all stitching is complete, mount and frame your picture (see page 103 for advice).

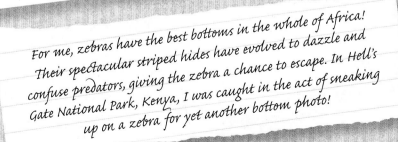
For me, zebras have the best bottoms in the whole of Africa! Their spectacular striped hides have evolved to dazzle and confuse predators, giving the zebra a chance to escape. In Hell's Gate National Park, Kenya, I was caught in the act of sneaking up on a zebra for yet another bottom photo!

Zebras 71

72 Zebras

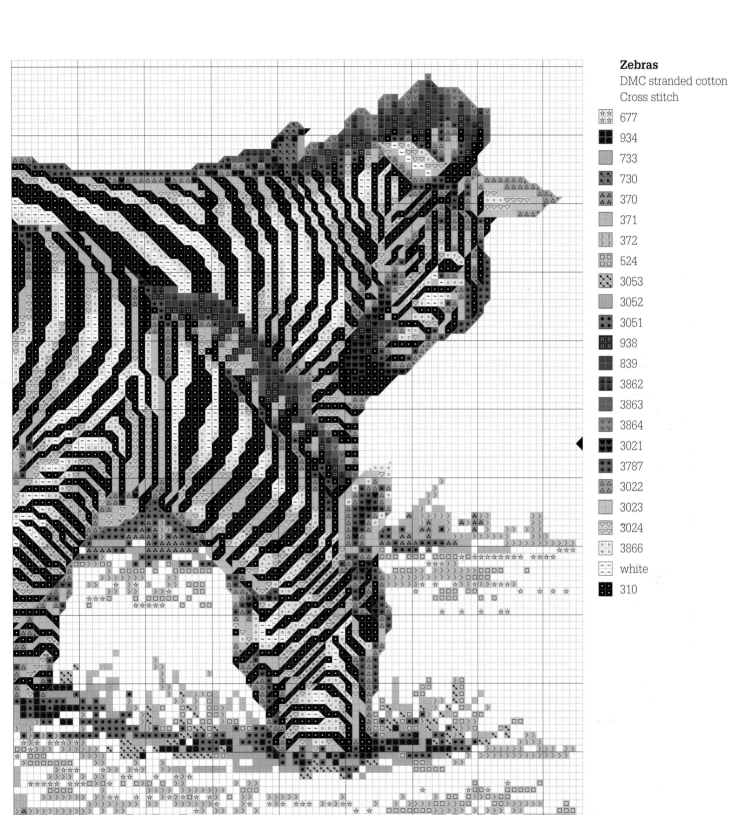

Zebras
DMC stranded cotton
Cross stitch

⛝	677
■	934
▨	733
⛝	730
⛝	370
▨	371
◫	372
⊞	524
⛝	3053
▨	3052
⛝	3051
⛝	938
■	839
⛝	3862
▨	3863
▨	3864
⛝	3021
⛝	3787
△	3022
▨	3023
♡	3024
◌	3866
⬚	white
■	310

Gorilla

Mountain gorillas can be seen in their natural habitat in Uganda. Each gorilla group, which can number up to 40 with females and young, has a dominant male, the silverback. These gentle giants usually avoid danger by quietly walking away in single file into the thick forest. The silverback will threaten interlopers with barks and stares, and ultimately will charge at them. Of all the primates, gorillas have to eat the most plant material to get the nutrients they need, which explains their pot bellies. An adorable baby gorilla peeking out from behind foliage has the most appealing eyes. Young gorillas stay with their mothers for about four years, until she has her next birth.

Lovable Baby

Stitch count 120 x 150
Design size 22 x 27.5cm (8½ x 10¾in)

You will need

- 35.5 x 40.5cm (14 x 16in) cream 14-count Aida
- DMC stranded cotton (floss) as listed in chart key (1 skein of each colour and 2 skeins of 3799 and 310)
- Tapestry needle size 24–26

Prepare your fabric and mark the centre point (see page 100). Work outwards from the centre of the chart overleaf. Work over one block of Aida, using two strands of stranded cotton (floss) for all cross stitch. Work the backstitch/long stitch with one strand of 3864 for the grass detail. If preferred, you could work French knots in two strands to replace the 677 cross stitches for the grass seed heads. Once all stitching is complete, mount and frame your picture (see page 103 for advice).

Nature is a wondrous thing; even the trees manipulate the animals by tempting them with tasty fruits. Gorillas, along with other creatures, come to feast on fruit that has fallen from the tree canopy, and thus play their part in seed dispersal and the regeneration of the African forests.

76 Gorilla

Gorilla

DMC stranded cotton
Cross stitch

648			
543		677	
3864		471	
3863		470	
3861		469	
3860		936	
779		832	
762		834	
415		3013	
318		3012	
414		3011	
317		934	
413		3348	
3799		3347	
433		3346	
801		3345	
938		895	
3371		645	
white		646	
310		647	

Gorilla 77

Giraffes

Noble is the word that comes to mind when I think of giraffes. Their fluid movement and bearing gives the impression they are never in a rush. Only when they are drinking have I seen them nervous – understandable as it is such an awkward manoeuvre. In the golden light of late afternoon we saw three young giraffes approach a pool to drink, shuffling forwards, backwards, sideways, before spreading their front legs wide and stooping to drink. But within seconds they were up and in flight, their gracefulness completely absent. Only after this was repeated several times, did an adult join them to drink, which seemed to have a calming effect.

All Grace and Elegance

Stitch count 180 x 110
Design size 33 x 20cm (13 x 7¾in)

You will need

- 46 x 33cm (18 x 13in) khaki 14-count Aida
- DMC stranded cotton (floss) as listed in chart key (1 skein of each colour)
- Tapestry needle size 24–26

Prepare your fabric and mark the centre point (see page 100). Work outwards from the centre of the chart overleaf. Work over one block of Aida, using two strands of stranded cotton (floss) for all cross stitch. Once all stitching is complete, mount and frame your picture (see page 103 for advice).

There are nine subspecies of giraffe, each with a recognisable skin pattern. They are browsers, feeding mainly on acacia leaves and other shoots and fruits. Their colouring might fade over the years, but those glorious patterned coats never do.

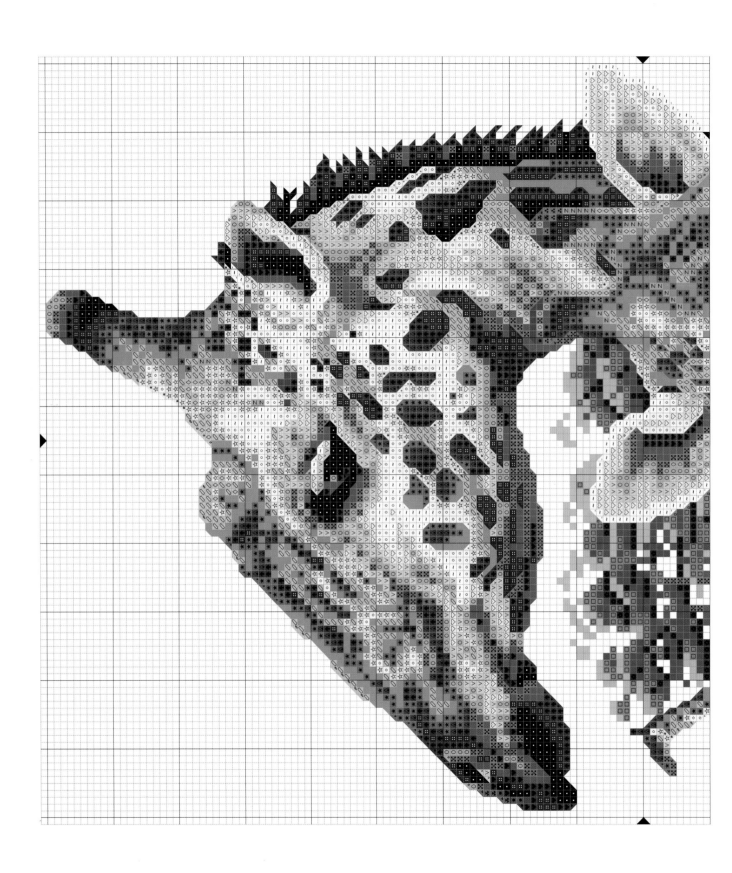

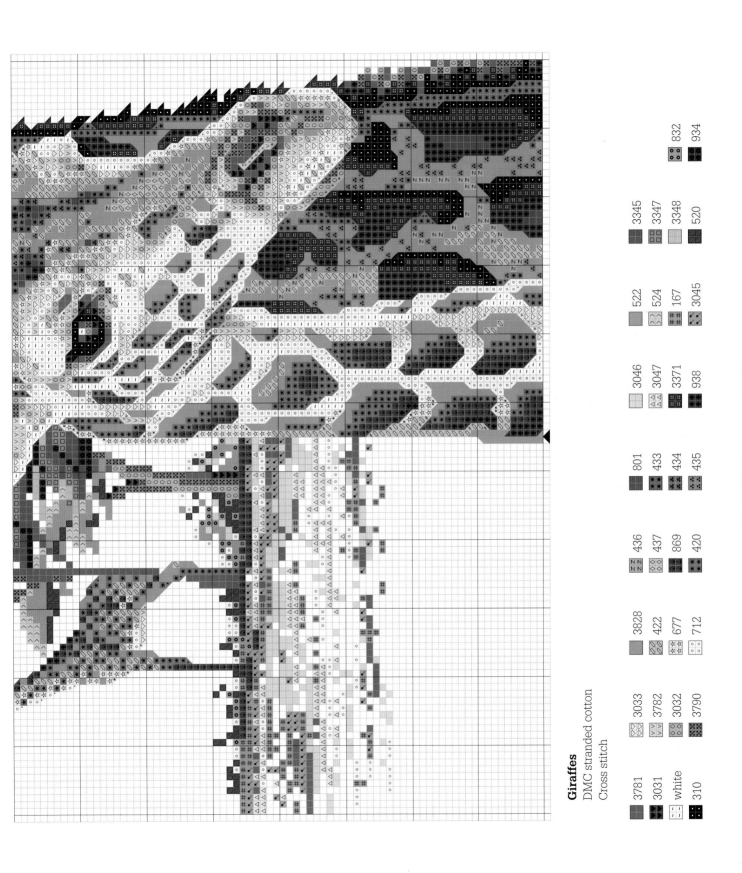

Giraffes

DMC stranded cotton
Cross stitch

3781	3033	3828
3031	3782	422
white	3032	677
310	3790	712

436	801	3046
437	433	3047
869	434	3371
420	435	938

522	3345	832
524	3347	934
167	3348	
3045	520	

Meerkats

What delightful creatures meerkats are. They are also called suricates and live in family groups or gangs, active in the daytime and very sociable. We saw them early in the morning, where they sunbathed before going off to forage, the young in hot pursuit of the older group members for tasty morsels, as they learned what to eat. While most of the gang members forage, some act as lookouts. These sentries find a vantage point and watch for threats, ready to call a warning to the others, so they can all dive for cover.

The Lookout

Stitch count 200 x 200
Design size 36.5 x 36.5cm (14¼ x 14¼in)

You will need
- 51 x 51cm (20 x 20in) cream 14-count Aida
- DMC stranded cotton (floss) as listed in chart key (1 skein of each colour and 2 skeins of 3033, 3032 and 3782)
- Tapestry needle size 24–26

Prepare your fabric and mark the centre point (see page 100). Work outwards from the centre of the chart on pages 84–87, over one block of Aida, using two strands of stranded cotton (floss) for all cross stitch. Work French knots with one strand of white for eye highlights. Once all stitching is complete, mount and frame your picture (see page 103 for advice).

The heat of an African afternoon made painting difficult at times – the paint drying on the brush before I could get it to the paper – so I often worked pencil drawings instead, making notes on details and colours for my paintings.

84 Meerkats

Meerkats
DMC stranded cotton
Cross stitch

676	840	610	580	832	3046	3828	738	3790	white
3866	839	611	581	834	3047	422	739	3032	310
842	938	612	829	167	869	677	3031	3782	
841	801	613	831	3045	420	712	3781	3033	

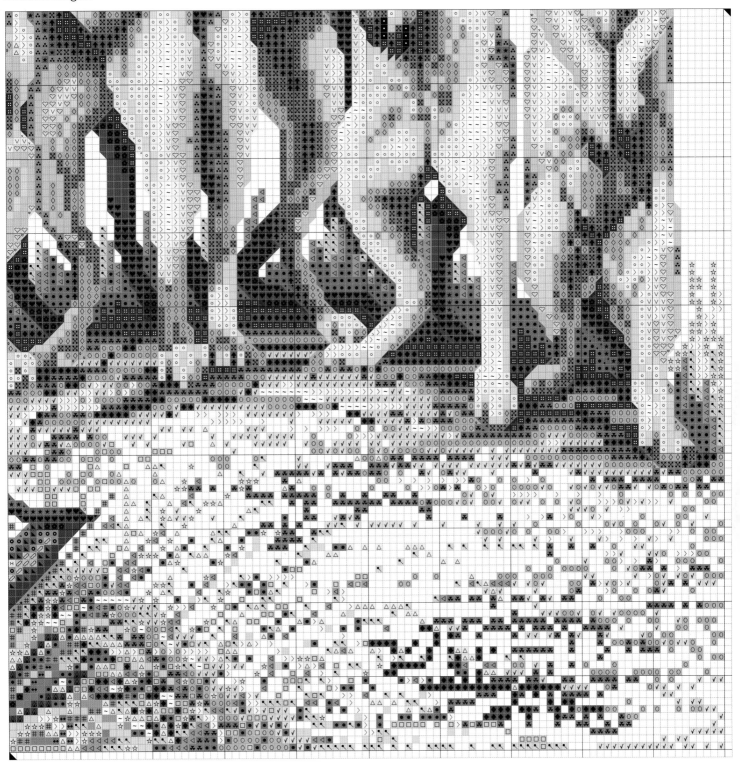

Meerkats
DMC stranded cotton
Cross stitch

	676		840		610		580		832		3046		3828		738		3790		white
	3866		839		611		581		834		3047		422		739		3032		310
	842		938		612		829		167		869		677		3031		3782		
	841		801		613		831		3045		420		712		3781		3033		

Safari Moments

This classic collection, which is a reminder to me of our wonderful trip, features six of the most well-known creatures on the African plains – elephant, ostrich, leopard, lioness, hippopotamus and crocodile. In this selection of small cameos I have included an elephant with a lot more attitude. The leopard and lioness deserved a second pose, while the ostrich, hippos and crocodile come high on the list of animals you long to see on a safari, though I chose to show a baby crocodile rather than an adult, which is a fearsome creature to me. The designs in this section are smaller and quicker to stitch so would make perfect gifts and greetings cards for family and friends. The elephant adorns a striking album cover, followed by two attractive cards featuring an impressive ostrich and a beautiful leopard in a classic pose, surveying her territory from a tree. Three other designs – a lioness stalking her prey, some fun hippo heads and a cute baby crocodile – can be stitched and made up in any way you chose. For example, the lioness would look superb worked on a smaller count fabric and mounted on a photo album cover, while the crocodile and hippos would make lovely cards or small framed pictures.

Charging Elephant

Stitch count 80 x 65
Design size 13 x 10cm (5 x 4in)

You will need
- 25.5 x 23cm (10 x 9in) natural 16-count Aida
- DMC stranded cotton (floss) as listed in chart key (1 skein of each colour)
- Tapestry needle size 24–26
- Photo album or journal
- Fabric to cover the album
- Craft glue
- Rickrack braid or other embellishments

Prepare your fabric and mark the centre point (see page 100). Work outwards from the centre of the chart on page 97, over one block of Aida, using two strands of stranded cotton (floss) for cross stitch. Work the backstitch with one strand: black for the tail and 938 for the foreground detail. Once all stitching is complete, frame the embroidery as a picture or mount it on to a photo album, as described on page 103.

Ostrich – the Biggest Bird

Stitch count 110 x 64
Design size 13 x 7.5cm (5 x 3in)

You will need

- 25.5 x 20cm (10 x 8in) cream 22-count Aida
- DMC stranded cotton (floss) as listed in chart key (1 skein of each colour)
- Tapestry needle size 24–26
- Double-fold card with aperture to fit embroidery
- Double-sided tape

Prepare your fabric and work outwards from the centre of the chart on page 98. Work over one block of Aida, using two strands of stranded cotton (floss) for all cross stitch. Once all stitching is complete, mount into a double-fold card (see page 103). Alternatively, mount and frame the design as a little picture.

The largest of all birds is unmistakable, and though only black and white there is nothing dull about an ostrich. The wings are small and they can't fly but we saw them running with great speed and endurance.

Leopard at Ease
Stitch count 70 x 85
Design size 9.5 x 12cm (3¾ x 4¾in)

You will need

- 25.5 x 28cm (10 x 11in) sky blue 18-count Aida
- DMC stranded cotton (floss) as listed in chart key (1 skein of each colour)
- Tapestry needle size 24–26
- Double-fold card with aperture to fit embroidery
- Double-sided tape

Prepare your fabric and work outwards from the centre of the chart on page 96. Work over one block of Aida, using two strands of stranded cotton (floss) for all cross stitch. Work backstitch with one strand of black for the face detail. Work a French knot in one strand of white for the eye highlight. Once all stitching is complete, mount into a double-fold card (see page 103). Alternatively, mount and frame the design as a picture.

When out on a game drive, straining eyes are scanning every tree, looking for a sign of a stashed carcass or the leopard itself. What gave this beauty away in this instance was a lazily swishing tail.

This lioness has her attention firmly fixed on the job of hunting. Several lionesses working together will carefully work their way around a herd, selecting the weakest animal and setting up their position. The end comes quickly for the unfortunate prey.

Lioness Gaze

Stitch count 70 x 90
Design size 13 x 16.5cm (5 x 6½in)

You will need
- 25.5 x 30.5cm (10 x 12in) light khaki 14-count Aida
- DMC stranded cotton (floss) as listed in chart key (1 skein of each colour)
- Tapestry needle size 24–26

Prepare your fabric and work outwards from the centre of the chart on page 95. Work over one block of Aida, using two strands of stranded cotton (floss) for all cross stitch. Work the backstitch with one strand: black for the eye and 869 for the backstitch/long stitch grass detail. Work a French knot in one strand of 3033 for the eye highlight. Once complete, mount and frame as a picture or in another way of your choice.

Hippo Heads

Stitch count 40 x 90
Design size 7.5 x 16.5cm (3 x 6½in)

You will need
- 20 x 30.5cm (8 x 12in) sage green 14-count Aida
- DMC stranded cotton (floss) as listed in chart key (1 skein of each colour)
- Tapestry needle size 24–26

Prepare your fabric and work outwards from the centre of the chart on page 95. Work over one block of Aida, using two strands of stranded cotton (floss) for all cross stitch. Once complete, mount and frame as a picture or in another way of your choice.

We saw hippos in the South Luangwa National Park, Zambia. At first the lake looked empty, completely covered with lush green water plants, then suddenly up came the heads. In a few minutes they were gone again – not even a hole in the vegetation to show they were there.

Baby Crocodile

Stitch count 41 x 90
Design size 7.5 x 16.5cm (3 x 6½in)

You will need

- 20 x 30.5cm (8 x 12in) blue 14-count Aida
- DMC stranded cotton (floss) as listed in chart key (1 skein of each colour)
- Tapestry needle size 24–26

Prepare your fabric and work outwards from the centre of the chart on page 96. Work over one block of Aida, using two strands of stranded cotton (floss) for all cross stitch. Work backstitch with one strand of black for eyes and mouth detail. Once complete, mount and frame as a picture or in another way of your choice.

A baby crocodile is delightful. Its mother, hearing its chirp as it is about to hatch, digs him out of the nest with the other siblings, gently carrying them in her mouth to the water.

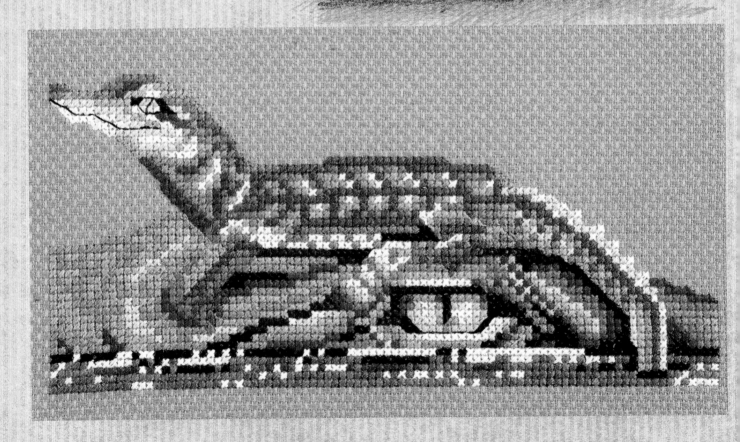

Lioness Gaze
DMC stranded cotton
Cross stitch

⬚⬚	739
△△	738
◹◹	437
♡♡	436
☆☆	435
⬢⬢	434
■	433
■■	801
■	938
▦	3371
⬚⬚	white
■	310
✳✳	869
◉◉	420
✦✦	3828
▨	422
◇◇	677
♥♥	3781
▦	3790
◈◈	3032
∨∨	3782
◦◦	3033
ⅠⅠ	712

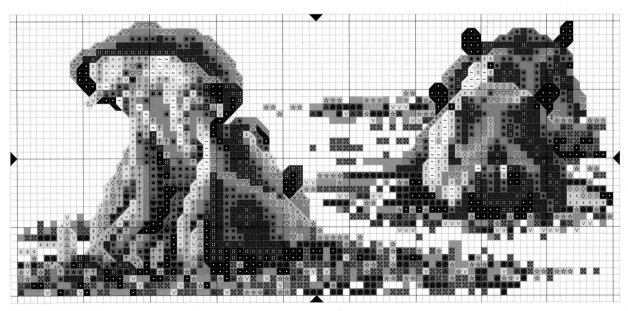

Hippo Heads
DMC stranded cotton
Cross stitch

↑↑	152	◇◇	415	✶✶	317	⬚⬚	white	■	934	▨	580	♥	3781	▨	3722
◦◦	225	▨	318	■	413	■	310	☆☆	165	△△	422	▲	3790
ⅠⅠ	762	■	414	▦	3799	■■	801	■	581	∨∨	677	◈◈	221

Safari Moments 95

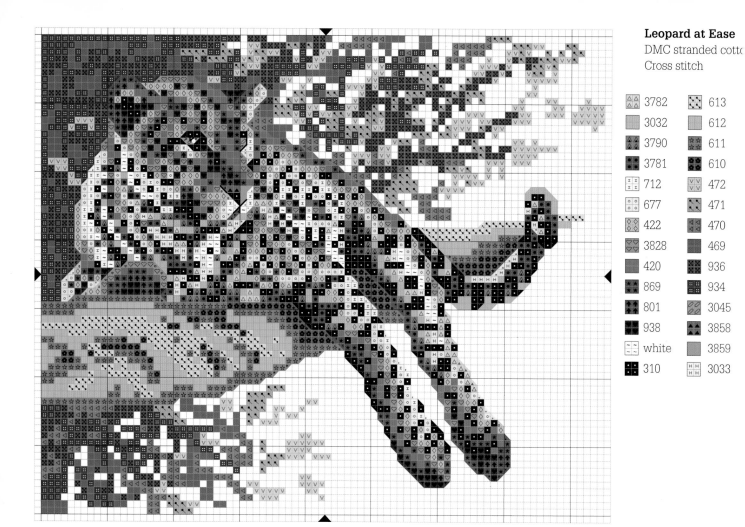

Leopard at Ease
DMC stranded cotton
Cross stitch

3782		613
3032		612
3790		611
3781		610
712		472
677		471
422		470
3828		469
420		936
869		934
801		3045
938		3858
white		3859
310		3033

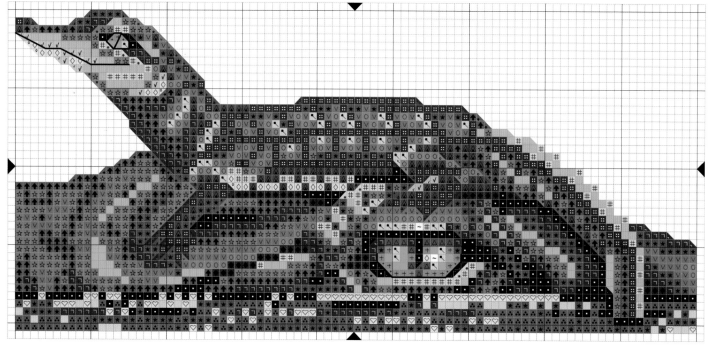

Baby Crocodile
DMC stranded cotton
Cross stitch

869	648	611	white	927	938	829	3829
413	3072	612	310	924	831	676	
3799	610	613	928	3371	830	729	

Charging Elephant
DMC stranded cotton
Cross stitch

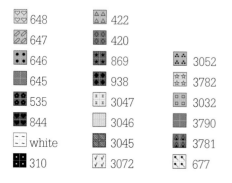

648	422
647	420
646	869	3052
645	938	3782
535	3047	3032
844	3046	3790
white	3045	3781
310	3072	677

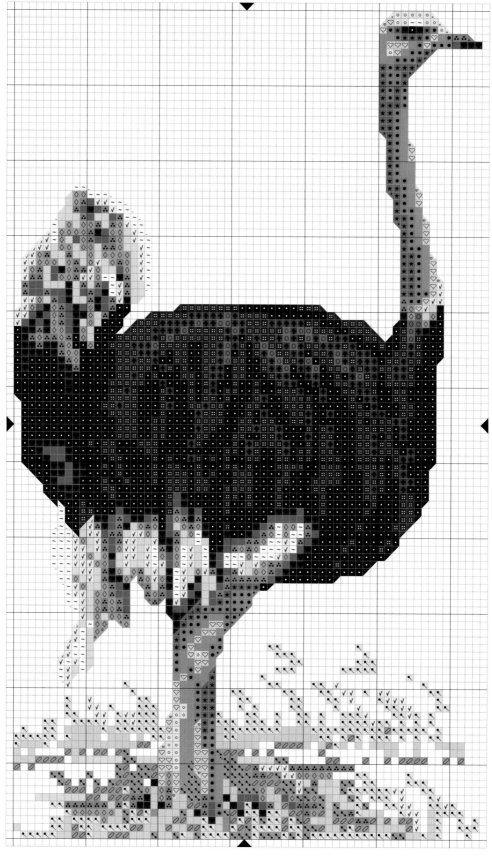

Ostrich
DMC stranded cotton
Cross stitch

642	413	632	3774	167
644	3799	3772	3021	3045
822	white	407	3787	3046
317	310	950	640	3047

Workbox

This section gives you all the information you will need to produce perfect cross stitch embroidery and successfully recreate the projects in this book. There is advice on materials and equipment, embroidery techniques, stitches and making up methods.

Materials and Equipment

This short section describes the basic materials and equipment you will need to stitch the designs in this book.

Fabrics

Most of the designs in this book have been worked on Aida fabric, which is stitched over one block. The main size used is 14 blocks or threads to 1in (2.5cm), often called 14-count. Some designs use an evenweave fabric such as linen, which should be worked over two threads. The same design stitched on fabrics of different counts will work up as different sizes. The larger the count, the more threads per 1in (2.5cm), therefore the smaller the finished design, and vice versa. Each project lists the type of fabric used, giving the thread count and fabric name. All DMC threads and fabrics are available from good needlework shops (see Suppliers for details).

Threads

If you want your designs to look the same as those shown in the photographs in this book, you will need to use the colours and threads listed for each project. I've used DMC stranded cotton (floss) but if you prefer Anchor threads, ask for a DMC–Anchor conversion table at your local needlecraft store. Some projects can be stitched with tapestry wool (yarn) instead, especially those worked just in cross stitch (see Using Tapestry Canvas overleaf).

It is best to keep threads tidy and manageable with thread organizers and

project cards. Cut the threads to equal lengths and loop them into project cards with the thread shade code and colour key symbol noted at the side. This will help prevent threads becoming tangled and codes being lost.

Stranded cotton (floss) This is the most widely used embroidery thread and is available in hundreds of colours, including silver and gold metallic. It is made from six strands twisted together to form a thick thread, which can be used whole or split into its thinner strands. The type of fabric used will determine how many strands of thread you use: most of the designs in this book use two strands for cross stitch and one for backstitch.

Tapestry wool (yarn) DMC wool is a matt, hairy yarn made from 100 per cent wool fibres twisted together to make a thick single thread, which cannot be split. If a design is worked using tapestry wool then it is usually stitched on a canvas using one or two strands of wool.

A wide selection of wool colours is available, with shades tending to be slightly duller than stranded cotton. There are conversion lists for colour matching from stranded cotton to tapestry yarn – ask at your needlecraft shop.

Needles

Stitch your cross stitch designs using a tapestry needle, which has a large eye and a blunt end to prevent damage to the fabric. Choose a size of needle that will slide easily through the fabric holes without distorting or enlarging them.

Scissors

You will need sharp embroidery scissors for cutting threads and good dressmaking scissors for cutting fabric.

Embroidery Frames

Your work will be easier to handle and stitches will be kept flat and smooth if you mount your fabric on an embroidery hoop or frame that will accommodate the whole design. Bind the outer ring of a hoop with a white bias tape to prevent it from marking the fabric. This will also keep the fabric taut and prevent it from slipping whilst you are working. Avoid placing a hoop over worked cross stitches.

Basic Techniques

The following techniques and tips will help you attain a professional finish by showing you how to prepare for work, work the stitches and care for your embroidery.

Preparing Fabric

Spending a little time preparing your embroidery fabric for work is a good idea, helping to avoid mistakes and produce superior finished results.

Fabric sizes Make sure you are using the correct size of fabric by checking the stitch count (the number of stitches across the height and width of the design) and design size given with each project. Each project gives the finished size of a design when worked on the recommended fabric, together with the amount of fabric needed. The overall fabric size should be at least 8–12.5cm (3–5in) larger than the finished size of the design to allow for turnings or seam allowances when mounting the work or making it up. To prevent fabric from fraying, machine stitch around the edges or bind with tape. Measurements are given in metric with imperial equivalent in brackets. Always use either metric or imperial – do not mix the two.

Centre point Starting your stitching from the centre point of the fabric ensures you will have enough fabric all round the design. To find the centre point, tack (baste) a row of stitches horizontally and vertically from the centre of each side of the fabric. These lines correspond to the arrows at the side of each chart and will cross at the centre point. Remove tacking once the embroidery is complete.

Using Charts

All the designs in this book use DMC embroidery fabrics and stranded cotton (floss). The colours and symbols shown on the chart keys correspond to DMC shade codes. Each coloured square on the chart represents one complete cross stitch and some squares also have a symbol. The colours and symbols correspond to those in the key beside each chart. A small triangle in a corner of a grid square represents a three-quarter cross stitch. French knots are shown by a coloured dot – the project instructions specify what thread shade to use. Solid coloured lines indicate backstitch or long stitch – refer to project instructions for details. The optional use of beads on a design will be in the instructions and will also specify which colours they replace.

Small black arrows at the side of a chart indicate the centre, and by lining these up you can find the centre point. Some of the charts are spread over four pages with the key repeated on each double page. Work systematically so you read the chart accurately and avoid mistakes. Constantly check your progress against the chart and count the stitches as you go. If your sight is poor you may find it helpful to enlarge a chart on a colour photocopier.

Using Tapestry Canvas

Many of the projects can also be stitched on canvas with tapestry wool (yarn) – perfect for more hard-wearing items such as doorstops, rugs and wall hangings. Ask at your local needlework shop for a conversion list to change stranded cotton (floss) colours to wool (yarn). Remember that when working on canvas you will also need a complementary background wool colour to fill in the canvas area around the design.

There is a range of canvas available in craft shops, from lighter weights used for embroidery to heavier canvas used for rugs. Canvas is basically of two types – tapestry and embroidery, as mono and interlock. Tapestry and embroidery canvases are ideal if the design has whole and three-quarter cross stitches or half and quarter cross stitches. Mono and interlock are ideal if the design has all whole cross stitch or half cross stitch.

When altering the count a design is stitched on, remember the design size will change so you need to work out carefully what size canvas is required. The stitch count will tell you how many stitches there are to every 2.5cm (1in). All of the projects have design sizes and stitch counts listed. Simply divide the stitch count by the fabric or canvas count to calculate the size of the design area, without any allowance. Always be generous with allowances, as you can trim the excess off. When working on canvas, add at least 13–15cm (5–6in) allowance all the way around a design.

Washing and Pressing Embroidery

If your work has become grubby during stitching, gently hand wash it in warm water using a mild liquid detergent. Do not rub or wring the embroidery. If necessary, use a soft nail brush to gently remove any stubborn marks. Rinse in clean water and then place the damp fabric on a clean white towel and leave to dry on a flat surface.

When ironing cross stitch embroidery, do not iron directly on your embroidery as this will flatten the stitches, remove the sheen from the threads and spoil the finished effect. Lay the work face down on a thick, clean white towel, cover with a clean, fine cloth and press carefully with a medium iron, taking extra care with any beads or metallic threads.

The Stitches

This section shows how to work the stitches used in the book. When following these instructions, note that stitching is over one block of Aida or two threads of evenweave.

Starting and Finishing Thread

To start off your first length of thread, make a knot at one end and push the needle through to the back of the fabric, about 2.5cm (1in) from your starting point, leaving the knot on the right side. Stitch towards the knot, securing the thread at the back of the fabric as you go (Fig 1). When the thread is secure, cut off the knot.

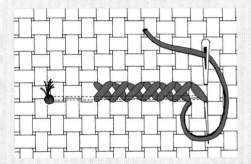

Fig 1 Starting to stitch

To finish off a thread or start new threads, simply weave the thread into the back of several stitches (Fig 2).

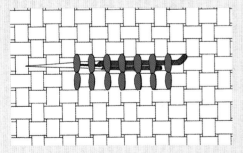

Fig 2 Finishing off a thread

Backstitch

Backstitch is indicated on the charts by a solid coloured line. It is worked around areas of completed cross stitches to add definition, or on top of stitches to add detail.

To work backstitch (Fig 3), pull the needle through the hole in the fabric at 1 and back through at 2. For the next stitch, pull the needle through at 3, then push to the back at 1, and repeat the process to make the next stitch. If working backstitch on an evenweave fabric, work each backstitch over two threads.

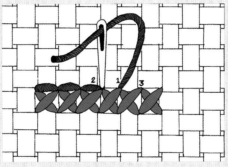

Fig 3 Working backstitch

Cross Stitch

Each coloured square on a chart represents one complete cross stitch. Cross stitch is worked in two easy stages. Start by working one diagonal stitch over one block of Aida (Fig 4) or two threads of evenweave (Fig 5), and then work a second diagonal stitch over the first stitch, but in the opposite direction to form a cross.

Fig 4 A cross stitch on Aida fabric

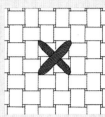

Fig 5 A cross stitch on evenweave fabric

Cross stitches can be worked in rows if you have a large area to cover. Work a row of half cross stitches in one direction and then back in the opposite direction with the diagonal stitches to complete each cross. The upper stitches of all the crosses should lie in the same direction to produce a neat effect (Fig 6).

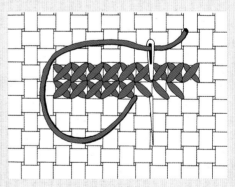

Fig 6 Working cross stitch in two journeys

Half Cross Stitch

This stitch is used if you chose to work a design on canvas in tapestry wool (yarn), replacing whole cross stitches with half stitches. A half cross stitch is simply one half of a cross stitch, with the diagonal facing the same way as the upper stitches of each complete cross stitch (Fig 7).

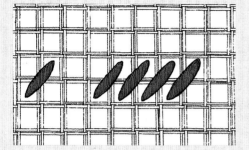

Fig 7 Working half cross stitch

Quarter Cross Stitch

If you chose to work a design on a double mesh canvas using wool (yarn), a quarter cross stitch should be used instead of a three-quarter cross stitch. To work, start at one corner of the canvas mesh and work in the same direction as any half stitches but insert the needle at the corner of the square.

Three-Quarter Cross Stitch

A small coloured triangle taking up half a chart square represents a three-quarter cross stitch. Forming a fractional stitch is less accurate on Aida than on evenweave because the centre of the Aida block needs to be pierced.

Work the first half of a cross stitch in the normal way, then work the second diagonal stitch in the opposite corner but insert the needle at the centre of the cross, forming three-quarters of the complete stitch (Fig 8). A square showing two smaller coloured triangles in opposite corners indicates that two three-quarter cross stitches will have to be worked back to back, sharing holes.

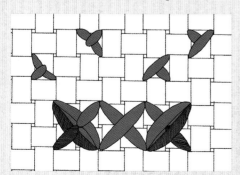

Fig 8 Working three-quarter cross stitch

French Knot

This is a small knot used for details, indicated on charts by coloured dots.

To work a French knot, bring the needle through to the front of the fabric, just above the point you want the stitch placed. Wind the thread once around the needle and, holding the twisted thread firmly, insert the needle a little way away from its starting position (Fig 9). Pull the thread through so the knot sits snugly on the fabric. Two tips for working French knots: never rush them and never go back into the same point where your thread came up or your knot will pull through to the back.

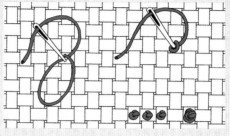

Fig 9 Working French knots

Long Stitch

These are used to work some animal whiskers and are indicated on charts by a straight coloured line – refer to the instructions for the colour. Work long stitches on top of cross stitches.

To work long stitch, pull the needle through the fabric at the point indicated on the chart and push it through at the other end shown on the chart, to make a long, straight stitch on top of the fabric. Repeat for the next stitch, carrying the thread across the back of the fabric to the next starting point (Fig 10).

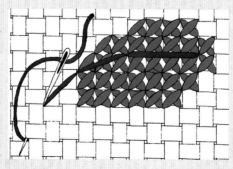

Fig 10 Working long stitch

Stitching Tips

- Steam press your embroidery fabric before you begin stitching, to remove any stubborn creases.
- Mount fabric on to an embroidery frame or hoop to keep stitches smooth and flat.
- For a neat appearance, work cross stitches with the top diagonals facing in the same direction.
- Thread up lengths of several colours of stranded cotton (floss) into separate needles, and arrange these at the side of your work by shade code or by key reference.
- Work the designs from the centre outwards, or split them into workable sections such as quarters. On larger designs, first work the main subject and then complete the background and surrounding designs.
- When taking threads across the back of a design, weave the thread through the back of existing stitches to avoid any ugly lines showing through on the right side of the work.
- Use short lengths of thread, about 30cm (12in), to reduce the likelihood of knotting and tangling.
- Check your progress constantly against the chart to avoid making counting mistakes.
- For smooth embroidery without lumps and bumps, avoid using knots at the back, and cut off any excess threads as short as possible.
- Keep your work clean by packing it away in its own clean plastic bag to prevent any accidents.

Making Up

This section describes how to make up the embroideries as illustrated, although the designs are simple to adapt and use in many different ways.

Mounting and Framing

It is best to take larger pictures to a professional framer, who will be able to stretch the fabric correctly and cut mounts accurately. If, however, you prefer to mount and frame yourself you will need a mitre box for cutting mitred corners on frames, some panel pins, a suitable saw, some hardboard (or thick card) and mount board. When choosing mount board and a frame, it is best to take your embroidery with you, to get an idea of what the end result will be.

Mount your embroidery on to thin hardboard or card and fasten by lacing it around the card or by stapling. Decide on the frame size you require and carefully cut your frame pieces to the correct size, then panel pin them together. Using a mount cutter or a craft or Stanley knife, cut your mount board to the required depth. Place the mount board into the frame, then the embroidery. Finally, cut hardboard to size for the backing and wedge in with metal clips or tape in place.

Using Ready-Made Items

Many of the projects in the book can be displayed in ready-made items such as firescreens and footstools, while the smaller designs in Safari Moments (pages 88–98) can be used in cards, trinket boxes and other smaller items. There are various manufacturers supplying such items (see Suppliers). Smaller pieces of embroidery can be backed with an iron-on interfacing (such as Vilene) to firm up the fabric and prevent wrinkling, and then be mounted in the item following the manufacturer's instructions.

Mounting Work in Cards

Double-fold cards with an aperture are readily available for embroidery from many outlets – see Suppliers. Trim the embroidery so it is slightly larger than the card aperture. Fix double-sided tape inside the card around the aperture, remove the backing from the tape and then press the embroidery on to the tape. The Framecraft cards I use already have this tape in place.

Photo Album

To mount embroidery on the front of a photo album, start by opening the album out flat and measuring it carefully, adding an allowance of 4cm (1½in) to the overall size. Cut your fabric to this size. Place the album centrally on the fabric, and working the front and back separately, spread fabric glue over the hard cover and then press the fabric in place, folding the edges over to the inside. Trim and glue the edges down into the spine of the album. Fold the corners over neatly and glue into place on the inside of the hard covers. Take the first and last page of the album and glue them down to cover the folded-in fabric.

If desired, create a frayed edge around your embroidery by removing threads around the edges. Glue your embroidery in place on the front of the journal, and then glue on other embellishments, such as rickrack braid, leaves and dried grasses.

Suppliers

If you should require any further information about products, catalogues, price lists or local stockists from any of the suppliers mentioned, contact them direct by post or phone. Remember to always include a stamped, addressed envelope. If contacting them by phone, they will be able to tell you if there is any charge for the catalogue or price lists.

UK

Coats Crafts UK
PO Box 22, Lingfield Estate, McMullen Road, Darlington, County Durham, DL1 1YQ
tel: 01325 394200 (consumer helpline)
For a wide range of needlework supplies, including Anchor threads

Craft Creations Ltd
Ingersoll House, Delamare Road, Cheshunt, Hertfordshire, EN8 9HD
tel: 01992 781900
email: enquiries@craftcreations.com
www.craftcreations.com
For card blanks and accessories

DMC Creative World
Pullman Road, Wigston, Leicester
LE18 2DY
tel: (0116) 281 1040
For threads and embroidery fabrics, and name and address of nearest DMC stockist

Framecraft Miniatures Ltd
Unit 3, Isis House, Lindon Road, Brownhills, West Midlands WS8 7BW
tel/fax (UK): 01543 360842
tel (international): 44 1543 453154
email: sales@framecraft.com
www.framecraft.com
For many ready-made items for embroidery, including cards

Impress Cards & Craft Materials
Slough Farm, Westhall, Suffolk, IP19 8RN
tel: 01986 781422
email: sales@impresscards.co.uk
www.impresscards.com
For ready-made card blanks and craft materials

For further information about Jayne Netley Mayhew's artwork visit her brother Ed's website: www.netzfineart.com

USA

Charles Craft Inc.
PO Box 1049, Laurenburg, NC 28353
tel: 910 844 3521
email: ccraft@carolina.net
www.charlescraft.com
For cross stitch fabrics and many useful pre-finished items

The DMC Corporation
South Hackensack Ave, Port Kearny, Building 10A, South Kearny, NJ 07032-4688
www.dmc-usa.com
For DMC threads and fabrics

Janlynn Corporation
2070 Westover Road, Chicopee, MA 01022
www.janlynn.com
For Jayne Netley Mayhew cross stitch kits

Mill Hill, a division of Wichelt Imports Inc.
N162 Hwy 35, Stoddard WI 54658
tel: 608 788 4600
fax: 608 788 6040
email: millhill@millhill.com
www. millhill.com
For Mill Hill beads and a US source for Framecraft products

Zweigart/Joan Toggit Ltd
262 Old Brunswick Road, Suite E, Piscataway, NJ 08854-3756
tel: 732 562 8888
email: info@zweigart,com
www.zweigart.com
For cross stitch fabrics

Acknowledgments

Thank you to my husband Ian for his patient understanding while I worked on this book, and his support and photographic skills.

A very special thank you to each of the following people, for their tremendous hard work, their care and the endless knowledge that they imparted to us:
Kenya's Masai Mara – Douglas Mugambi, Robert Mulandi and Joshua Mutie.
Kenya to Zambia – Christopher Ncube, Njabula Sibanda (known to us as JB) and Johannes Sibanda.

Thanks to John Parkes of Outpost Trading, who still smiles when I arrive with my embroideries to be framed at the last moment. A big thank you to Cara Ackerman at DMC and Sarah Carlton-Gray at Framecraft Miniatures Ltd for their support.

Thanks also to the following people for their contributions and help with getting this book published. Doreen Montgomery for her invaluable support. Cheryl Brown for having the same idea at the same time as I did for this book. Linda Clements for her absolutely invaluable help perfecting my text. To Prudence Rogers and Charly Bailey for the beautiful book design and to Jennifer Proverbs for getting everyone organized. To Kim Sayer for the wonderful photography and my husband Ian for the evocative snapshots throughout.

Index

Pages in **bold** indicate charts

About the Author

Jayne Netley Mayhew is a renowned wildlife artist and cross stitch designer. She takes her inspiration from nature and her designs are detailed and varied, from eagles and dolphins to lions and zebras. Her work features regularly in needlecraft and needlework magazines and is also available from Janlynn Kits and DMC.

© Chris Mayhead